The Editor

GRACE IOPPOLO is the founder and director of the Henslowe-Alleyn Digitisation Project and is Professor of Shakespearean and Early Modern Drama in the Department of English and American Literature at the University of Reading, England. She is the author of *Dramatists and Their Manuscripts in the Age of Shakespeare, Jonson, Middleton and Heywood: Authorship, Authority, and the Playhouse* (2006) and *Revising Shakespeare* (1991). She has edited Shakespeare's *King Lear* for Norton and has published widely on textual transmission, the history of the book, and literary and historical manuscripts, most recently as the co-editor of *Elizabeth I and the Culture of Writing* (2007). She is the General Editor of *The Collected Works of Thomas Heywood*, forthcoming 2012–15.

A NORTON CRITICAL EDITION

William Shakespeare
MEASURE FOR MEASURE

AN AUTHORITATIVE TEXT

SOURCES

CRITICISM

ADAPTATIONS AND RESPONSES

Edited by

GRACE IOPPOLO
UNIVERSITY OF READING

W • W • NORTON & COMPANY • *New York* • *London*

Contents

Illustrations

Introduction

This is a play as full of genius as it is of wisdom.
—William Hazlitt

It is a hateful work, although Shakespearian throughout.
—S. T. Coleridge

Since its composition in 1604, *Measure for Measure* has divided readers and theatrical audiences as well as literary critics. For those who demand that their Shakespeare serve not just as artist and playwright but as moral guide and spiritual leader, the play's conclusion shows the failure of theater to educate and redeem society. For those who expect their Shakespeare to be complex, contradictory, and ultimately unknowable, the play's conclusion demonstrates the power of theater to challenge and change culture. Either way, Shakespeare succeeded at the midpoint of his career in producing a "magnificent" play, to use Algernon Swinburne's term, that questions traditional dramatic genres, characters, structures, and themes precisely because the conclusion fails definitively to resolve them.

In writing this play, Shakespeare may not have been concerned with the demands and expectations of future generations of audiences but with one particular audience member on December 26, 1604—King James I, who had become the financial patron of Shakespeare's acting company in 1603. As the official theatrical representatives of James's artistic vision, the King's Men were invited to perform plays at court to celebrate holidays, and in 1604 on St. Stephen's Day, traditionally associated with the rich giving alms to the poor, *Measure for Measure* was staged before James in the banqueting hall in Whitehall Palace in London. As J. W. Lever argues, Shakespeare closely recalled events at James's court in 1603 and 1604 in this play, including the king's displeasure at the "exuberance" of his subjects in greeting him on his processions through his kingdom. But in writing *Measure for Measure*, Shakespeare also appears to have drawn heavily on James's own artistic composition, *Basilkon Doron* (Greek; The King's Gift), first published in 1599 and reissued in 1603. In Book 2 of this conduct manual, written to advise his oldest son and heir, Prince Henry, on the political and moral responsibilities of kingship, James focuses on how to ensure that his people have access to "justice and equitie."

ix

have been inserted verbatim in *Measure for Measure*, as in this warning: "Feare no uproars for doing of justice, since yee may assure your selfe, the most part of your people will ever naturally favour justice: providing always, that ye doe it onely for love to justice, and not for satisfying any particular passions of yours." Although Angelo fails spectacularly in the proviso to not satisfy any particular passion in doing justice, Shakespeare leaves it ambiguous as to whether the Duke succeeds in acting only "for love to justice," as the successive "uproars" in the trial scene throughout Act 5 demonstrate.

Basilkon Doron may at first appear to offer a series of traditional platitudes, especially in such statements as: "Cherish no man more than a good Pastor, hate no man more than a proude Puritan." In *Measure for Measure*, it is the pseudo-pastor, the Duke, who exposes the evils of the proud Puritan, Angelo, even as both come to learn that they, like Isabella, profess a moral absolutism that hides emotional and psychological frailties. But if Shakespeare mocks such simplistic statements, he seems to have recognized James's political

The figure of Chastity from Trevelyon's *Miscellany* (1608).

Measure for Measure is far more than a staged version of *Basilikon Doron,* and Shakespeare's necessary flattery of his new patron is only one small part of the play's foundation. As seems to have been his pattern, Shakespeare drew on a variety of sources in writing this play, demonstrating that he continually reworked basic genres, plots, structures, characters, and themes until he could shape *Measure for Measure* into a coherent whole that would not allow strict boundaries or interpretations. The play's most obvious source is George Whetstone's 1578 play *The History of Promos and Cassandra,* in which the magistrate Promos, of the dominions of Hungary and Bohemia, uses a "severe" but "little regarded" law to prosecute Andrugio and his willing lover for fornication. Andrugio's sister, the virtuous Cassandra, unsuccessfully pleads to Promos for Andrugio's release and eventually agrees to sleep with Promos to save her brother's life. After Promos has, he thinks, had Andrugio executed, he commands his jailer to send Andrugio's head to Cassandra. Devastated by the loss of her brother and her virginity, she appeals to the king, who, horrified by her tale, forces Promos to marry Cassandra and afterward sentences him to execution. Cassandra, now "tyed in the greatest bondes of affection to her husband," pleads for Promos's life, which is granted once Andrugio, whose life had secretly been spared by the Jailer, reveals himself to his sister and all those assembled, including the king. Promos and Andrugio are forgiven their crimes and, presumably, go on to live happily with their wives.

While Shakespeare drew heavily on Whetstone's play, he also seems to have kept in mind an episode in Cinthio's prose romance *Hecatommithi* (1565) and his adaptation of it in the play *The Tragedy of Epitia* (1583), which relate the story of Epitia's agreement to sleep with the Austrian magistrate Juriste, who has prosecuted her brother Vico for raping an unwilling virgin. Nonetheless, Juriste has Vico executed, and Epitia complains to the emperor, who orders Juriste to marry Epitia, who then pleads for her husband's life to be spared, and the emperor agrees. Cinthio's play adds a number of extra characters and also has Vico's life secretly spared, as becomes apparent at the end. Thus, between the two versions of his story, Cinthio reworked the degree, consequences, and relative value of Juriste's crimes, possibly because the genre of drama required a more appealing and less culpable villain than a prose romance. While Whetstone probably used Cinthio's works to write his play, it is not clear if Shakespeare did the same or had Cinthio's stories filtered through Whetstone's texts. However, Shakespeare did use stories in *Hecatommithi* as sources for *Othello* and possibly other plays.

At least two analogues, both prose texts, of the basic *Measure for Measure* plot exist. The first is Thomas Lupton's *The Second Part of Too Good to Be True* (1581), which presents the story of "a notorious lines). Because of these linguistic difficulties, some critics have suggested that the text of *Measure for Measure* was mangled in its first printing in the 1623 First Folio, either because it had suffered cuts or because a later adapter had misjudged where to insert alterations. However, as this distraction in language brilliantly mirrors the distraction in thought of many of the characters, Shakespeare may have more closely succeeded in transmitting into print the words that he composed in manuscript than has been previously recognized.

In *Measure for Measure*, Shakespeare pushed beyond the usual limits not just of language but of religion. His sympathetic reconsideration and reinstitution of the old religion, Catholicism, in a post-Reformation age suggests recklessness, for the play insists on the goodness of Catholic friars and nuns and depends on the emotional consolation offered by their precepts and institutions. During the reign of Queen Elizabeth I, who quashed numerous conspiracies to overthrow her by Catholics, including her cousin Mary Queen of Scots, nostalgic representations of the old religion on stage would have provoked a great deal of controversy. But by 1604, Mary's son and heir James I had begun to explore the reconciliation of the two religions, allowing clergy to debate such questions as whether grace (or religious mercy) is grace, despite of all controversy, and which types and degrees of sin grace could pardon or alleviate. Whether Shakespeare was sentimentally looking back at his youth in Stratford (where there remained some practice of the old faith in the 1560s and 1570s) or agitating for the primacy of Catholicism in his adulthood is impossible to know for certain. Instead the play offers scope for a variety of interpretations. At the very least, Shakespeare's reconsideration of St. Matthew's maxim to "judge not, that ye be not judged. For with what judgment ye judge, ye shall be judged, and with what measure you mete, it shall be measured to you again" demands that Christianity prove its relevance to early modern England.

The play's genre, unfortunately labeled first a "dark comedy" by eighteenth-century critics and then a "problem comedy" by the respected critic Frederick S. Boas in 1896, seems designed stubbornly to resist any type of definition or labeling. A further problem is Shakespeare's apparent refusal to place an obvious climax in the third act, as the classical five-act structure dictates. But *Measure for Measure* marks the point in Shakespeare's career when he had abandoned patriotic English history plays based on chronicles and tragedies deriving from Greek, and outdated, formulas. By 1603, the beginning of the Jacobean age marked by James's ascension to the throne, Shakespeare also seemed to have become bored with traditional "festive" comedies such as *The Comedy of Errors*, *As You Like It*, *Much Ado about Nothing*, and *A Midsummer Night's Dream*, in which one the success of such theatrically forced marriages. But if the Duke seems outrageous in matching couples who are ill-suited, unwilling, or unbalanced in measures of love, kindness, or goodness, how outrageous must Shakespeare himself look when he has thus far made a career of doing the same in his "festive comedies." If audiences feel uncomfortable with the play's ending, as the three centuries of critics included in this volume claim, Shakespeare succeeds in emphasizing that audiences must not be passive but active and complicit. Shakespeare provides the interpretations but his audiences must provide the judgments, measure for measure.

Coleridge and other eighteenth- and nineteenth-century critics called the play "hateful" for its sometimes explicit rendering of sexuality, as in the obscene comments of Pompey and Lucio and the lascivious behavior of Angelo, and for the lack of severe punishment for so many criminals. In the twentieth century, critics complained instead about the play's problematic portrayals of the Duke, Angelo, and Isabella but excused them, as G. Wilson Knight did, by strictly framing them within the Christian gospels of St. Matthew and St. Luke. In expanding *Measure for Measure* beyond a simple Christian allegory and praising its "wonderful vitality," critics such as Rosalind Miles still believed in 1970 that *Measure for Measure* "remains only partially successful" because it deprives audiences of "the sense of harmony and completeness," as Swinburne and A. C. Bradley had argued. Now labeled by such critics as Kathleen McLuskie and Jonathan Dollimore as the "patriarchal," if not the misogynistic, bard, Shakespeare's faulty gender constructions and the disorder they create are seen as the source of early- and mid-twentieth-century commentators' judgments of Isabella as "cold," "selfish," and "sexually frigid" for her failure to save her brother by sleeping with Angelo. With the rise of feminist and new historical approaches to the play, Isabella has been more sympathetically interpreted as the victim of sexual harassment. Yet Isabella's willingness to act as bawd to Mariana and as assistant to the pimp-like Duke in setting up the bed trick suggests that she is no feminist icon; nor is the Duke, who forces Juliet to confess that her sin of fornication is "heavier" than Claudio's but later advises Mariana that "'tis no sin" for her to consummate her relationship with Angelo. Like the Duke and Angelo, Isabella is incapable of weighing others with herself; all three see themselves as living in an exclusive and cloistered world of the mind (and "complete" or closed bosom) in which Mistress Overdone's employees and customers do not exist, rather than in a communal, physical world of the body and the senses, in which bawds, prostitutes, and tapsters make a tidy income.

Whether Isabella silently accepts the Duke's hasty proposal depends on a number of factors, including if the audience is made to see the basic, it produces confusion about male and female identity, as Elbow, the symbol of inept justice, amply testifies. If Shakespeare began to question in *Measure for Measure* whether marriage was designed not to sanction sexuality between men and women but to prevent sexuality between men and between women, he further explored this topic in the plays that he wrote shortly afterward, including *Othello*, *Macbeth*, *Pericles*, *Cymbeline*, and *The Winter's Tale*. This may explain why Coleridge found the play "hateful" but "Shakespearean" throughout.

With such dangerous subconscious desires lurking beneath the conscious surface of "decorum," to use the Duke's word in Act 1, Scene 4, it is not surprising that Restoration audiences preferred adaptations of *Measure for Measure* to the original. The first was *The Law against Lovers* (1662), William D'Avenant's lighthearted combination of this play and *Much Ado about Nothing*, in which Angelo wishes only to test Isabella's virtue and not to force her into bed, thereby earning her love and her hand in marriage. The second was Charles Gildon's less drastic redaction, *Measure for Measure, or, Beauty the Best Advocate* (1700), which offers Isabella more opportunity to fall in love with the Duke before his proposal. However, Shakespeare's text, purged of its seeming vulgarities, was staged repeatedly in the eighteenth and nineteenth centuries with such celebrated actors as John Philip Kemble, Sarah Siddons, and W. C. Macready, and throughout the twentieth century, with the text largely restored, with Charles Laughton, John Gielgud (in a memorable production directed by Peter Brook), Ian Richardson, and Judi Dench, among many others. Charles Marowitz, known for his savage, postmodern adaptations of Shakespeare's plays, is not totally convincing in his version of *Measure for Measure* (1975) in portraying Isabella's rape by Angelo as an abhorrent event, especially as that scene and the closing scene in which the "Bishop" and "Angelo" joke about abuse provide a level of titillation and voyeurism that would make many uncomfortable. But perhaps this is Marowitz's point: the original play is much less obvious in making men and women confront the probability that their sexual fears are in fact their sexual desires but eventually forces them to do so.

There is no record of *Measure for Measure's* performance between that on December 26, 1604, and the close of the theaters in 1642, although it almost certainly was in the King's Men repertory for some years and performed both at the outdoor, public Globe theater and the indoor, private Blackfriars theater, where dimmable lighting could emphasize the play's insistence on physical, and moral, "shadows," "darkness," and "lightness." No matter the venue, if the play finally fails to deliver an absolute moral message, Shakespeare, who exposes the follies of moral absolutism throughout *Measure for Measure*, has

The Text of
MEASURE FOR MEASURE

Measure for Measure

Dramatis Personae

VINCENTIO, the Duke
ANGELO, the Deputy
ESCALUS, an ancient Lord
CLAUDIO, a young Gentleman
LUCIO, a Fantastic   5
Two other like GENTLEMEN
PROVOST
THOMAS, a Friar
PETER, a Friar
A JUSTICE   10
ELBOW, a simple Constable
FROTH, a foolish Gentleman
POMPEY, Servant to Mistress Overdone
ABHORSON, an Executioner
BARNARDINE, a dissolute Prisoner   15
[VARRIUS, a Gentleman]
ISABELLA, Sister to Claudio
MARIANA, betrothed to Angelo
JULIET, beloved of Claudio
FRANCISCA, a nun   20
MISTRESS OVERDONE, a bawd
      Lords, Gentlemen, Officers, Servants, Citizens, a Boy

THE SCENE: Vienna.

---

1. **VINCENTIO:** This name appears only in this list and was probably supplied by the scribe Ralph Crane (probably in consultation with King's Men's actors).
3. **ancient:** elderly.
5. **LUCIO:** His name puns on the Latin word for "light" (*luce*) as well as *Lucifer*, the devil, whose name became a synonym for a "match," i.e., fire.
   Fantastic: person who is fantastical in speech, action, or dress.
7. **PROVOST:** officer charged with dealing with criminals.
21. **bawd:** woman who procures customers for prostitutes.

3

That to th'observer doth thy history
Fully unfold. Thyself and thy belongings
Are not thine own so proper as to waste   30
Thyself upon thy virtues, they on thee.
Heaven doth with us as we with torches do,
Not light them for themselves, for if our virtues
Did not go forth of us, 'twere all alike
As if we had them not. Spirits are not finely touched   35
But to fine issues, nor nature never lends
The smallest scruple of her excellence
But, like a thrifty goddess, she determines
Herself the glory of a creditor,
Both thanks and use. But I do bend my speech   40
To one that can my part in him advertise.
Hold, therefore, Angelo:
In our remove be thou at full ourself.
Mortality and mercy in Vienna
Live in thy tongue and heart! Old Escalus,   45
Though first in question, is thy secondary.
Take thy commission.
ANGELO   Now, good my lord,
Let there be some more test made of my metal
Before so noble and so great a figure
Be stamped upon it.
DUKE   No more evasion.   50
We have with a leavened and preparèd choice
Proceeded to you; therefore take your honors.
Our haste from hence is of so quick condition
That it prefers itself, and leaves unquestioned
Matters of needful value. We shall write to you,   55
As time and our concernings shall importune,
How it goes with us, and do look to know
What doth befall you here. So, fare you well.
To th'hopeful execution do I leave you
Of your commissions.

29–35. **Thyself . . . not:** alluding to the biblical Parable of the Talents (Matthew 25:14–30).
  40. **bend:** turn.
  41. **advertise:** i.e., fulfill.
  43. **remove:** absence.
  46. **question:** seniority; **secondary:** subordinate.
  47. **Take thy commission:** The Duke here hands Angelo a written commission or order.
  48. **metal:** basis for making a "stamped" coin, with pun on *mettle,* a variant spelling of *metal* as "character" or "ability."
  51. **leavened:** developed.
  56. **importune:** urge.

SECOND GENTLEMAN   Amen.

LUCIO   Thou conclud'st like the sanctimonious pirate, that
went to sea with the ten commandments, but scraped one
out of the table.

SECOND GENTLEMAN   "Thou shalt not steal"?   10

LUCIO   Ay, that he razed.

FIRST GENTLEMAN   Why? 'Twas a commandment to command
the captain and all the rest from their functions: they put
forth to steal. There's not a soldier of us all that, in the
thanksgiving before meat, do relish the petition well that   15
prays for peace.

SECOND GENTLEMAN   I never heard any soldier dislike it.

LUCIO   I believe thee, for I think thou never wast where grace
was said.

SECOND GENTLEMAN   No? A dozen times at least.   20

FIRST GENTLEMAN   What? In meter?

LUCIO   In any proportion, or in any language.

FIRST GENTLEMAN   I think, or in any religion.

LUCIO   Ay, why not? Grace is grace, despite of all controversy,
as, for example, thou thyself art a wicked villain, despite of   25
all grace.

FIRST GENTLEMAN   Well, there went but a pair of shears
between us.

LUCIO   I grant: as there may between the lists and the velvet.
Thou art the list.   30

FIRST GENTLEMAN   And thou the velvet. Thou art good velvet;
thou'rt a three-piled piece, I warrant thee. I had as lief be a
list of an English kersey as be piled, as thou art piled, for a
French velvet. Do I speak feelingly now?

LUCIO   I think thou dost, and, indeed, with most painful   35
feeling of thy speech. I will, out of thine own confession,
learn to begin thy health, but, whilst I live, forget to drink
after thee.

---

11. **razed:** scratched out.
15. **thanksgiving:** grace before meals.
24. **Grace . . . controversy:** probably alluding to a series of contemporary arguments
among Protestant clerics on whether to accept or reject the pre-Reformation (and Catholic) dogma that grace (or mercy) could alleviate particular sins; **despite:** in spite of.
27. **shears:** scissors.
29. **lists:** cheap fabric edgings; **velvet:** luxurious French fabric with a nap, leading to a series
of puns on the physical consequences of the English losing their "nap," or hair, from the
treatment for the "French" disease, or syphilis.
32. **three-piled piece:** most luxurious velvet, with a pun on *balding*; **lief:** gladly.
33. **kersey:** coarse cloth; **piled:** bald.
34. **French:** i.e., sexually diseased; **feelingly:** to the point, with a pun on *painfully* as a
result of being sexually diseased.
37. **begin:** begin a toast to.

Lucio (Ian Richardson) encounters Mistress Overdone (Norah Blayney) in Act 1, Scene 2, of the 1962 Royal Shakespeare Company production.

FIRST GENTLEMAN   But most of all agreeing with the   75
    proclamation.
LUCIO   Away! Let's go learn the truth of it.
                  Exeunt LUCIO [*and* GENTLEMEN].
MISTRESS OVERDONE   Thus, what with the war, what with the
    sweat, what with the gallows, and what with poverty, I am
    custom-shrunk.   80

---

79. sweat: sweating sicknesses (including that arising from venereal disease).
80. custom-shrunk: shrunken in customer numbers.

Act 1, Scene 3

Enter PROVOST, CLAUDIO [*bound*], JULIET,
OFFICERS, LUCIO *and two* GENTLEMEN.

CLAUDIO   Fellow, why dost thou show me thus to th'world?
Bear me to prison, where I am committed.
PROVOST   I do it not in evil disposition,
But from Lord Angelo by special charge.
CLAUDIO   Thus can the demi-god, Authority,   5
Make us pay down for our offence by weight
The words of heaven; on whom it will, it will;
On whom it will not, so, yet still 'tis just.
LUCIO   Why, how now, Claudio? Whence comes this restraint?
CLAUDIO   From too much liberty, my Lucio, liberty.   10
As surfeit is the father of much fast,
So every scope by the immoderate use
Turns to restraint. Our natures do pursue,
Like rats that ravin down their proper bane,
A thirsty evil, and when we drink we die.   15
LUCIO   If I could speak so wisely under an arrest, I would
    send for certain of my creditors, and yet, to say the truth, I
    had as lief have the foppery of freedom as the morality of
    imprisonment. What's thy offence, Claudio?
CLAUDIO   What but to speak of would offend again.   20
LUCIO   What, is't murder?
CLAUDIO   No.
LUCIO   Lechery?
CLAUDIO   Call it so.
PROVOST   Away, sir, you must go.   25
CLAUDIO   One word, good friend: Lucio, a word with you.
LUCIO   A hundred, if they'll do you any good. Is lechery so
    looked after?
CLAUDIO   Thus stands it with me: upon a true contract
I got possession of Julietta's bed;   30
You know the lady, she is fast my wife,

1.3. Location: the same.
  5. demi-god: minor or inferior deity.
  9. restraint: shackling.
11. surfeit: excess.
14. ravin down: devour; bane: poison.
18. lief: gladly; foppery: foolishness.
28. looked after: watched.
29. true contract: genuine contract; clandestine marriages, considered legal, could consist
    of such simple pledges between a couple.
31. fast: firmly fixed as.

And there receive her approbation.
Acquaint her with the danger of my state,
Implore her, in my voice, that she make friends
To the strict deputy. Bid herself assay him;   65
I have great hope in that, for in her youth
There is a prone and speechless dialect
Such as move men. Beside, she hath prosperous art
When she will play with reason and discourse,
And well she can persuade.   70

LUCIO   I pray she may, as well for the encouragement of the
         like, which else would stand under grievous imposition, as
         for the enjoying of thy life, who I would be sorry should be
         thus foolishly lost at a game of tick-tack. I'll to her.

CLAUDIO I thank you, good friend Lucio.   75

LUCIO   Within two hours.

CLAUDIO Come, officer, away.   *Exeunt.*

Act 1, Scene 4

Enter DUKE *and* FRIAR THOMAS.

DUKE   No, holy father, throw away that thought,
        Believe not that the dribbling dart of love
        Can pierce a complete bosom. Why I desire thee
        To give me secret harbor hath a purpose
        More grave and wrinkled than the aims and ends   5
        Of burning youth.

FRIAR   May your grace speak of it?

DUKE   My holy sir, none better knows than you
        How I have ever loved the life removed,
        And held in idle price to haunt assemblies
        Where youth, and cost, witless bravery keeps.   10

----

62. **approbation:** confirmation.
63. **state:** condition.
65. **assay:** try.
67. **prone . . . dialect:** mercy-provoking and wordless language (with unintentional pun on *prone* as "sexually available").
68. **move:** persuade (with an unintentional bawdy pun on *arousing*).
72. **like:** same; **grievous imposition:** serious order.
74. **tick-tack:** i.e., backgammon game in which pegs were inserted in holes (with a bawdy pun).
1.4. Location: a monastery in Vienna.
   2. **dribbling:** i.e., unable to wound; **dart of love:** alluding to Cupid, whose arrows provoked sudden love in those struck by them.
   3. **complete:** full, possibly with an unintentional pun on *closed* or *covert* (see 5.1.11).
   8. **removed:** cloistered; see note at 1.1.67–70.
   9. **assemblies:** large groups of people.
  10. **witless:** foolish.

I will, as 'twere a brother of your order,
Visit both prince and people. Therefore, I prithee,   45
Supply me with the habit, and instruct me
How I may formally in person bear
Like a true friar. Moe reasons for this action
At our more leisure shall I render you;
Only, this one: Lord Angelo is precise,   50
Stands at a guard with envy, scarce confesses
That his blood flows, or that his appetite
Is more to bread than stone. Hence shall we see,
If power change purpose, what our seemers be.   *Exeunt.*

Act 1, Scene 5

Enter ISABELLA *and* FRANCISCA, *a nun.*

ISABELLA   And have you nuns no farther privileges?
FRANCISCA   Are not these large enough?
ISABELLA   Yes, truly; I speak not as desiring more,
    But rather wishing a more strict restraint
    Upon the sisterhood, the votarists of Saint Clare.   5
LUCIO (*within*)   Hoa! Peace be in this place!
ISABELLA   Who's that which calls?
FRANCISCA   It is a man's voice. Gentle Isabella,
    Turn you the key, and know his business of him;
    You may, I may not; you are yet unsworn.
    When you have vowed, you must not speak with men   10
    But in the presence of the prioress;
    Then, if you speak, you must not show your face,
    Or, if you show your face, you must not speak.
    He calls again: I pray you answer him.   [*Exit* FRANCISCA.]
ISABELLA   Peace and prosperity! Who is't that calls?   15

---

44. **brother:** friar, which is a corruption of *frère,* the French word for "brother." Unlike monks who were cloistered and devoted to a contemplative life, friars were required to derive financial support from and live among the larger community.
47. **bear:** bear myself.
48. **Moe:** more.
50. **precise:** strict and inflexible.
51. **Stands at a guard:** i.e., keeps watch.
1.5. Location: a nunnery in Vienna.
   1. **farther:** larger.
   5. **votarists:** followers of (i.e., nuns); **Saint Clare:** 13th-century Italian saint.
  11. **prioress:** head of the order.

ISABELLA   Adoptedly, as school-maids change their names
By vain though apt affection.
LUCIO   She it is.
ISABELLA   O, let him marry her!
LUCIO   This is the point.
The Duke is very strangely gone from hence,   50
Bore many gentlemen, myself being one,
In hand and hope of action. But we do learn,
By those that know the very nerves of state,
His giving-out were of an infinite distance
From his true-meant design. Upon his place,   55
And with full line of his authority,
Governs Lord Angelo, a man whose blood
Is very snow-broth; one who never feels
The wanton stings and motions of the sense,
But doth rebate and blunt his natural edge   60
With profits of the mind, study, and fast.
He, to give fear to use and liberty,
Which have, for long, run by the hideous law,
As mice by lions, hath picked out an act,
Under whose heavy sense your brother's life   65
Falls into forfeit. He arrests him on it,
And follows close the rigor of the statute
To make him an example. All hope is gone,
Unless you have the grace by your fair prayer
To soften Angelo. And that's my pith of business   70
'Twixt you and your poor brother.
ISABELLA   Doth he so
Seek his life?
LUCIO   Has censured him already,
And, as I hear, the Provost hath a warrant
For's execution.
ISABELLA   Alas! What poor
Ability's in me to do him good?   75

47. **change:** exchange.
48. **apt:** appropriate, normal.
51. **Bore:** i.e., deceived.
54. **giving-out:** official announcement.
55. **true-meant:** actual.
58. **snow-broth:** melted snow.
59. **wanton:** lustful; **motions . . . sense:** physical stirrings of sensuality.
60. **rebate:** reduce.
64. **act:** illegal act (here, singled out as an example).
66. **forfeit:** loss, due to the commission of a crime.
70. **pith:** essence.
72. **censured:** condemned.
74. **For's:** for his.

And pulled the law upon you.
ANGELO 'Tis one thing to be tempted, Escalus,
Another thing to fall. I not deny
The jury, passing on the prisoner's life,
May in the sworn twelve have a thief or two   20
Guiltier than him they try. What's open made to justice,
That justice seizes. What knows the laws
That thieves do pass on thieves? 'Tis very pregnant,
The jewel that we find, we stoop and take it,
Because we see it, but what we do not see   25
We tread upon, and never think of it.
You may not so extenuate his offence
For I have had such faults, but rather tell me,
When I, that censure him, do so offend,
Let mine own judgment pattern out my death,   30
And nothing come in partial. Sir, he must die.

                    Enter PROVOST.

ESCALUS   Be it as your wisdom will.
ANGELO   Where is the Provost?
PROVOST   Here, if it like your honor.
ANGELO   See that Claudio
Be executed by nine tomorrow morning.
Bring him his confessor, let him be prepared,   35
For that's the utmost of his pilgrimage.   [*Exit* PROVOST.]
ESCALUS   Well, heaven forgive him, and forgive us all!
Some rise by sin, and some by virtue fall.
Some run from brakes of ice, and answer none,
And some condemned for a fault alone.   40

            Enter ELBOW, FROTH, POMPEY, OFFICERS.

ELBOW   Come, bring them away! If these be good people in
    a commonweal that do nothing but use their abuses in
    common houses, I know no law! Bring them away!

19. **passing:** deliberating.
20. **twelve:** i.e., a jury of twelve men.
21. **open:** openly.
23. **pregnant:** evident or notable.
31. **nothing:** in nothing; **partial:** biased.
35. **confessor:** priest to hear confession (one of the Catholic Church's sacraments).
38. **Some . . . fall:** This line is in italics in the Folio text, suggesting that the Provost is quoting a proverbial expression.
39. **brakes:** traps.
41. **away:** error for *here.*
42. **commonweal:** commonwealth or population; **use:** carry out.
43. **common houses:** i.e., brothels.

ESCALUS   By the woman's means?

ELBOW   Ay, sir, by Mistress Overdone's means, but as she spit
in his face, so she defied him.   80

POMPEY   Sir, if it please your honor, this is not so.

ELBOW   Prove it before these varlets here, thou honorable
man, prove it.

ESCALUS [*To* ANGELO]   Do you hear how he misplaces?

POMPEY   Sir, she came in great with child, and longing—saving   85
your honor's reverence—for stewed prunes. Sir, we had but
two in the house, which at that very distant time stood, as
it were, in a fruit dish, a dish of some threepence—your
honors have seen such dishes, they are not China dishes,
but very good dishes—   90

ESCALUS   Go to, go to, no matter for the dish, sir.

POMPEY   No, indeed, sir, not of a pin, you are therein in the
right, but to the point. As I say, this Mistress Elbow, being, as
I say, with child, and being great-bellied, and longing, as I
said, for prunes, and having but two in the dish, as I said,   95
Master Froth here, this very man, having eaten the rest, as I
said, and, as I say, paying for them very honestly—for, as you
know, Master Froth, I could not give you threepence again—

FROTH   No, indeed.

POMPEY   Very well. You being then, if you be remembered,   100
cracking the stones of the foresaid prunes—

FROTH   Ay, so I did indeed.

POMPEY   Why, very well. I telling you then, if you be
remembered, that such a one and such a one were past cure
of the thing you wot of, unless they kept very good diet, as   105
I told you—

FROTH   All this is true.

POMPEY   Why, very well then.

ESCALUS   Come, you are a tedious fool. To the purpose: what
was done to Elbow's wife that he hath cause to complain   110
of? Come me to what was done to her.

---

79. **she:** Elbow's wife.
80. **his:** Pompey's.
82. **varlets:** error for *honorable men*; **honorable:** error for *dishonorable*.
84. **misplaces:** mistakes, in using the opposites of the intended words.
85. **great with child:** heavily pregnant.
86. **stewed prunes:** brothel fruit, with a pun on *stews*, or brothels; *prunes* has two sylla-
bles, hence the Folio spelling of "prewyns."
88. **of:** worth.
96. **Froth:** His name suggests that Froth "foams at the mouth" or speaks words of little
value.
101. **stones:** pits.
105. **wot:** know.

A 1791 illustration of Act 2, Scene 1, in which Pompey defends Froth to Escalus and Elbow.

ELBOW   First, an't like you, the house is a respected house;   150
  next, this is a respected fellow, and his mistress is a
  respected woman.
POMPEY   By this hand, sir, his wife is a more respected person
  than any of us all.

150. **an't**: if it; **respected**: error for *suspected*.
153. **hand**: Pompey is raising his hand in an attempt to swear officially.

FROTH   I thank your worship. For mine own part, I never
come into any room in a taphouse but I am drawn in.

ESCALUS   Well, no more of it, Master Froth. Farewell.

[*Exit* FROTH.]

Come you hither to me, Master Tapster. What's your
name, Master Tapster?   195

POMPEY   Pompey.

ESCALUS   What else?

POMPEY   Bum, sir.

ESCALUS   'Troth, and your bum is the greatest thing about
you, so that, in the beastliest sense, you are Pompey the   200
Great. Pompey, you are partly a bawd, Pompey, howsoever
you color it in being a tapster. Are you not? Come, tell me
true; it shall be the better for you.

POMPEY   Truly, sir, I am a poor fellow that would live.

ESCALUS   How would you live, Pompey? By being a bawd?   205
What do you think of the trade, Pompey? Is it a lawful trade?

POMPEY   If the law would allow it, sir.

ESCALUS   But the law will not allow it, Pompey, nor it shall
not be allowed in Vienna.

POMPEY   Does your worship mean to geld and splay all the   210
youth of the city?

ESCALUS   No, Pompey.

POMPEY   Truly, sir, in my poor opinion, they will to't then. If
your worship will take order for the drabs and the knaves,
you need not to fear the bawds.   215

ESCALUS   There is pretty orders beginning, I can tell you. It
is but heading and hanging.

POMPEY   If you head and hang all that offend that way but for
ten year together, you'll be glad to give out a commission for
more heads. If this law hold in Vienna ten year, I'll rent the   220
fairest house in it after threepence a bay. If you live to see
this come to pass, say Pompey told you so.

ESCALUS   Thank you, good Pompey, and, in requital of your
prophecy, hark you: I advise you, let me not find you before
me again upon any complaint whatsoever; no, not for   225
dwelling where you do. If I do, Pompey, I shall beat you

---

198. **Bum:** buttocks.
200–201. **Pompey the Great:** The real Pompey the Great (109–48 B.C.E.) was a great mil-
itary leader and later ruler of Rome in a triumvirate with Marcus Crassus and
Julius Caeasar.
210. **geld and splay:** castrate and spay, hence neuter.
214. **drabs and the knaves:** prostitutes and foolish men (i.e., customers).
217. **heading:** beheading.
221. **threepence a bay:** three pennies per area of a house, hence ludicrously cheap.

Act 2, Scene 2

Enter PROVOST [*and a*] SERVANT.

SERVANT   He's hearing of a cause; he will come straight.
I'll tell him of you.
PROVOST   Pray you do.   [*Exit* SERVANT.]
                                    I'll know
His pleasure; may be he will relent. Alas,
He hath but as offended in a dream!
All sects, all ages, smack of this vice, and he   5
To die for it?

Enter ANGELO.

ANGELO   Now, what's the matter, Provost?
PROVOST   Is it your will Claudio shall die tomorrow?
ANGELO   Did not I tell thee yea? Hadst thou not order?
Why dost thou ask again?
PROVOST   Lest I might be too rash.   10
Under your good correction, I have seen
When, after execution, judgment hath
Repented o'er his doom.
ANGELO   Go to; let that be mine.
Do you your office, or give up your place,
And you shall well be spared.   15
PROVOST   I crave your honor's pardon.
What shall be done, sir, with the groaning Juliet?
She's very near her hour.
ANGELO   Dispose of her
To some more fitter place, and that with speed.

[*Enter* SERVANT.]

SERVANT   Here is the sister of the man condemned   20
Desires access to you.
ANGELO   Hath he a sister?

2.2. Location: the Duke's palace in Vienna.
  1. **cause:** complaint.
  4. **He:** Claudio.
  5. **sects:** groups; **smack:** smell.
12–13. **judgment . . . doom:** i.e., after the execution of a prisoner, the judge regretted his
        decision to execute.
  14. **place:** position of provost.
  17. **groaning:** i.e., in labor.
  18. **hour:** hour of giving birth.

An 1803 illustration of Act 2, Scene 2, in which Isabella pleads to Angelo
to spare Claudio's life as Lucio listens.

ISABELLA   Yes: I do think that you might pardon him,
   And neither heaven nor man grieve at the mercy.
ANGELO   I will not do't.
ISABELLA   But can you if you would?
ANGELO   Look what I will not, that I cannot do.   55
ISABELLA   But might you do't, and do the world no wrong,
   If so your heart were touched with that remorse
   As mine is to him?
ANGELO   He's sentenced, 'tis too late.
LUCIO [To ISABELLA.]   You are too cold.
ISABELLA   Too late? Why, no! I that do speak a word   60
   May call it back again. Well believe this:

57. **remorse:** compassion.

LUCIO [*Aside*]   Ay, well said.   95
ANGELO   The law hath not been dead, though it hath slept.
  Those many had not dared to do that evil
  If the first that did th'edict infringe
  Had answered for his deed. Now 'tis awake,
  Takes note of what is done, and, like a prophet,   100
  Looks in a glass that shows what future evils—
  Either now, or by remissness new conceived,
  And so in progress to be hatched and born—
  Are now to have no successive degrees,
  But here they live to end.
ISABELLA   Yet show some pity.   105
ANGELO   I show it most of all when I show justice;
  For then I pity those I do not know,
  Which a dismissed offence would after gall,
  And do him right that, answering one foul wrong,
  Lives not to act another. Be satisfied: 110
  Your brother dies tomorrow. Be content.
ISABELLA   So you must be the first that gives this sentence,
  And he that suffers. O, it is excellent
  To have a giant's strength, but it is tyrannous
  To use it like a giant.   115
LUCIO [*Aside*]   That's well said.
ISABELLA   Could great men thunder
  As Jove himself does, Jove would ne'er be quiet,
  For every pelting petty officer
  Would use his heaven for thunder,   120
  Nothing but thunder. Merciful Heaven
  Thou rather with thy sharp and sulphurous bolt
  Splits the unwedgeable and gnarlèd oak
  Than the soft myrtle. But man, proud man,
  Dressed in a little brief authority,   125
  Most ignorant of what he's most assured—
  His glassy essence—like an angry ape
  Plays such fantastic tricks before high heaven

101. **glass:** mirror (here, one that shows the future).
102. **remissness:** neglect or carelessness.
104. **degrees:** levels.
108. **gall:** irritate.
118. **Jove:** Roman king of the gods, possibly a substitution for *God*; the play was probably purged of words referring to God as a result of the 1606 Act Against Abuses.
119. **pelting:** paltry.
123. **unwedgeable:** incapable of being split; **gnarlèd:** twisted.
127. **glassy essence:** transparent soul.
128. **fantastic:** extraordinary or unbelievable.

Ere sunrise, prayers from preservèd souls,   160
From fasting maids, whose minds are dedicate
To nothing temporal.
ANGELO   Well, come to me tomorrow.
LUCIO [*To* ISABELLA]   Go to, 'tis well. Away!
ISABELLA   Heaven keep your honor safe!
ANGELO [*Aside.*]   Amen,
For I am that way going to temptation,   165
Where prayers cross.
ISABELLA   At what hour tomorrow
Shall I attend your lordship?
ANGELO   At any time 'fore noon.
ISABELLA   'Save your honor!
                        [*Exeunt* LUCIO, ISABELLA, PROVOST.]
ANGELO   From thee, even from thy virtue!
What's this? What's this? Is this her fault or mine?   170
The tempter or the tempted, who sins most? Ha?
Not she, nor doth she tempt, but it is I
That, lying by the violet in the sun,
Do as the carrion does, not as the flower,
Corrupt with virtuous season. Can it be   175
That modesty may more betray our sense
Than woman's lightness? Having waste ground enough,
Shall we desire to raze the sanctuary,
And pitch our evils there? O, fie, fie, fie!
What dost thou? Or what art thou, Angelo?   180
Dost thou desire her foully for those things
That make her good? O, let her brother live!
Thieves for their robbery have authority
When judges steal themselves. What, do I love her,
That I desire to hear her speak again   185
And feast upon her eyes? What is't I dream on?
O cunning enemy, that, to catch a saint,
With saints dost bait thy hook! Most dangerous
Is that temptation that doth goad us on
To sin in loving virtue. Never could the strumpet,   190

160. **preservèd:** i.e., heavenly.
161. **dedicate:** dedicated.
166. **cross:** i.e., cannot help.
168. **'Save:** God save.
173. **violet:** flower that symbolizes purity.
174. **carrion:** corpse.
175. **Corrupt . . . season:** become foul through supposedly virtuous power.
176. **sense:** (1) sensuality; (2) sense or understanding.
177. **lightness:** promiscuity.
178. **raze:** destroy.
190. **strumpet:** whore.

JULIET   Yes, as I love the woman that wronged him.   25
DUKE   So then, it seems, your most offenceful act
  Was mutually committed?
JULIET   Mutually.
DUKE   Then was your sin of heavier kind than his.
JULIET   I do confess it, and repent it, father.
DUKE   'Tis meet so, daughter, but lest you do repent,   30
  As that the sin hath brought you to this shame—
  Which sorrow is always toward ourselves, not heaven,
  Showing we would not spare heaven as we love it,
  But as we stand in fear—
JULIET   I do repent me as it is an evil,   35
  And take the shame with joy.
DUKE   There rest.
  Your partner, as I hear, must die tomorrow,
  And I am going with instruction to him.
  Grace go with you! *Benedicite*!   *Exit.*
JULIET   Must die tomorrow! O, injurious law   40
  That respites me a life whose very comfort
  Is still a dying horror!
PROVOST   'Tis pity of him.   *Exeunt.*

Act 2, Scene 4

   Enter ANGELO.

ANGELO   When I would pray and think, I think and pray
  To several subjects. Heaven hath my empty words,
  Whilst my invention, hearing not my tongue,
  Anchors on Isabel: heaven in my mouth,
  As if I did but only chew his name,   5
  And in my heart the strong and swelling evil
  Of my conception. The state whereon I studied
  Is, like a good thing, being often read,
  Grown seared and tedious. Yea, my gravity,
  Wherein—let no man hear me—I take pride,   10

---

28. heavier: more serious (sins were graded by seriousness), with a pun on *pregnant*.
39. *Benedicite*: Bless you (Latin).
2.4. Location: the Duke's palace in Vienna.
  3. invention: imagination.
  5. chew: i.e., say without accepting.
  7. conception: idea or plan.
  9. seared: dried up; the Folio text reads *feard,* with the *f* probably an error for a handwritten "long s" in the manuscript copy used to print *F*.

ANGELO   Ha? Fie, these filthy vices! It were as good
　　To pardon him that hath from nature stolen
　　A man already made, as to remit
　　Their saucy sweetness that do coin heaven's image   45
　　In stamps that are forbid. 'Tis all as easy
　　Falsely to take away a life true made
　　As to put metal in restrainèd means
　　To make a false one.
ISABELLA   'Tis set down so in heaven, but not in earth.   50
ANGELO   Say you so? Then I shall pose you quickly.
　　Which had you rather, that the most just law
　　Now took your brother's life, or, to redeem him,
　　Give up your body to such sweet uncleanness
　　As she that he hath stained?
ISABELLA   Sir, believe this,   55
　　I had rather give my body than my soul.
ANGELO   I talk not of your soul; our compelled sins
　　Stand more for number than for accompt.
ISABELLA   How say you?
ANGELO   Nay, I'll not warrant that, for I can speak   60
　　Against the thing I say. Answer to this:
　　I, now the voice of the recorded law,
　　Pronounce a sentence on your brother's life;
　　Might there not be a charity in sin
　　To save this brother's life?
ISABELLA   Please you to do't,   65
　　I'll take it as a peril to my soul;
　　It is no sin at all, but charity.
ANGELO   Pleased you to do't, at peril of your soul,
　　Were equal poise of sin and charity.
ISABELLA   That I do beg his life, if it be sin,   70
　　Heaven let me bear it! You granting of my suit,
　　If that be sin, I'll make it my morn prayer
　　To have it added to the faults of mine,
　　And nothing of your answer.
ANGELO   Nay, but hear me.

---

44. remit: pardon or forgive.
45. saucy sweetness: wanton desire.
46. stamps: i.e., images.
48. metal . . . means: following the imagery in the previous lines of a coin being made from stamped metal; here the restrainèd means suggest counterfeiting.
51. pose: question.
57. compelled: i.e., collected in number.
58. accompt: account.
69. poise: weight.

Should die for ever.   110

ANGELO   Were not you then as cruel as the sentence
That you have slandered so?

ISABELLA   Ignominy in ransom and free pardon
Are of two houses: lawful mercy
Is nothing kin to foul redemption.   115

ANGELO   You seemed of late to make the law a tyrant,
And rather proved the sliding of your brother
A merriment than a vice.

ISABELLA   O, pardon me, my lord, it oft falls out
To have what we would have, we speak not what we mean.   120
I something do excuse the thing I hate
For his advantage that I dearly love.

ANGELO   We are all frail.

ISABELLA   Else let my brother die,
If not a fedary, but only he
Owe and succeed thy weakness.   125

ANGELO   Nay, women are frail too.

ISABELLA   Ay, as the glasses where they view themselves,
Which are as easy broke as they make forms.
Women? Help heaven! Men their creation mar
In profiting by them. Nay, call us ten times frail,   130
For we are soft as our complexions are,
And credulous to false prints.

ANGELO   I think it well,
And from this testimony of your own sex—
Since, I suppose, we are made to be no stronger
Than faults may shake our frames—let me be bold.   135
I do arrest your words. Be that you are,
That is, a woman; if you be more, you're none.
If you be one—as you are well expressed
By all external warrants—show it now
By putting on the destined livery.   140

ISABELLA   I have no tongue but one; gentle, my lord,
Let me intreat you, speak the former language.

---

110. **die for ever:** be subject to eternal damnation in hell (for committing the sin of
fornication).
113. **Ignominy in ransom:** ransom purchased from ignomy or shame.
124. **fedary:** accomplice.
125. **thy weakness:** the weakness that you point out.
127. **glasses:** mirrors.
132. **credulous:** apt to believe; **prints:** i.e., impressions.
136. **arrest:** accept at face value.
137. **more:** a woman; **none:** a virgin (hence a girl).
139. **warrants:** signs.
140. **destined livery:** expected clothing, i.e., act like a woman, not an asexual girl.

Angelo (Daniel Evans) exerts his authority over Isabella (Emma Fielding) in Act 2, Scene 4, of the 2003 Royal Shakespeare Company production.

Either of condemnation or approof,
Bidding the law make curtsey to their will,
Hooking both right and wrong to the appetite,
To follow as it draws! I'll to my brother.
Though he hath fallen by prompture of the blood,   180
Yet hath he in him such a mind of honor
That, had he twenty heads to tender down
On twenty bloody blocks, he'd yield them up
Before his sister should her body stoop
To such abhorred pollution.   185
Then, Isabel live chaste, and brother die:
More than our brother is our chastity.
I'll tell him yet of Angelo's request,
And fit his mind to death, for his soul's rest.   *Exit.*

176. **approof:** approval.
177. **make curtsey:** defer.
180. **prompture:** prompting.
187. **More . . . chastity:** the Folio text has the first word preceded by quotation marks, with no closing quotation marks, so Isabella, who uses the plural *our,* may be quoting a proverbial or other statement here.

For ending thee no sooner. Thou hast nor youth nor age,
But as it were an after-dinner's sleep,
Dreaming on both, for all thy blessèd youth
Becomes as aged, and doth beg the alms   35
Of palsied eld, and when thou art old and rich,
Thou hast neither heat, affection, limb, nor beauty
To make thy riches pleasant. What's yet in this
That bears the name of life? Yet in this life
Lie hid moe thousand deaths; yet death we fear   40
That makes these odds all even.
CLAUDIO   I humbly thank you.
     To sue to live, I find I seek to die,
     And, seeking death, find life. Let it come on.
ISABELLA (*Within*)   What, hoa? Peace here; grace and good
     company!
PROVOST   Who's there? Come in, the wish deserves a welcome.   45
DUKE   Dear sir, ere long I'll visit you again.
CLAUDIO   Most holy sir, I thank you.

                    Enter ISABELLA.

ISABELLA   My business is a word or two with Claudio.
PROVOST   And very welcome. Look, signior, here's your sister.
DUKE   Provost, a word with you.   50
PROVOST   As many as you please.
DUKE   Bring me to hear them speak where I may be concealed.
                              [DUKE *and* PROVOST *withdraw.*]
CLAUDIO   Now, sister, what's the comfort?
ISABELLA   Why,
     As all comforts are: most good, most good, indeed.   55
     Lord Angelo, having affairs to heaven,
     Intends you for his swift ambassador,
     Where you shall be an everlasting leiger.
     Therefore, your best appointment make with speed;
     Tomorrow you set on.
CLAUDIO   Is there no remedy?   60
ISABELLA   None, but such remedy as, to save a head,
     To cleave a heart in twain.
CLAUDIO   But is there any?

33. **after-dinner's:** mid-afternoon's.
35. **the alms:** money for the poor.
36. **eld:** old age.
40. **moe thousand:** a thousand more.
42. **sue:** plead.
58. **leiger:** permanent representative (*OED*).
62. **twain:** two.

In prenzie guards! Dost thou think, Claudio,
If I would yield him my virginity
Thou mightst be freed?
CLAUDIO   O heavens, it cannot be!
ISABELLA   Yes, he would give't thee, from this rank offence,
So to offend him still. This night's the time   100
That I should do what I abhor to name,
Or else thou diest tomorrow.
CLAUDIO   Thou shalt not do't.
ISABELLA   O, were it but my life,
I'd throw it down for your deliverance
As frankly as a pin.
CLAUDIO   Thanks, dear Isabel.   105
ISABELLA   Be ready, Claudio, for your death tomorrow.
CLAUDIO   Yes. Has he affections in him
That thus can make him bite the law by th'nose
When he would force it? Sure it is no sin,
Or of the deadly seven it is the least.   110
ISABELLA   Which is the least?
CLAUDIO   If it were damnable, he, being so wise,
Why would he for the momentary trick
Be perdurably fined? O Isabel!
ISABELLA   What says my brother?   115
CLAUDIO   Death is a fearful thing.
ISABELLA   And shamed life a hateful.
CLAUDIO   Ay, but to die, and go we know not where,
To lie in cold obstruction, and to rot,
This sensible warm motion to become   120
A kneaded clod, and the delighted spirit
To bathe in fiery floods or to reside
In thrilling region of thick-ribbed ice,
To be imprisoned in the viewless winds,
And blown with restless violence round about   125
The pendent world, or to be worse than worst
Of those that lawless and incertain thought
Imagine howling! 'Tis too horrible!
The weariest and most loathèd worldly life
That age, ache, penury, and imprisonment   130
Can lay on nature is a paradise

96. **prenzie gards:** i.e., lavish clothing that hides corruption.
113. **trick:** deception.
114. **perdurably:** enduringly.
120. **motion:** body.
121. **kneaded clod:** trodden-on clump of dirt in a grave.
126. **pendent:** hanging.
130. **penury:** poverty.

with hopes that are fallible; tomorrow you must die; go to
your knees and make ready.

CLAUDIO   Let me ask my sister pardon. I am so out of love with   170
life that I will sue to be rid of it.

DUKE   Hold you there. Farewell. Provost, a word with you.

PROVOST [*Comes forward*]   What's your will, father?

DUKE   That, now you are come, you will be gone. Leave me
a while with the maid; my mind promises with my habit no   175
loss shall touch her by my company.

  PROVOST   In good time. *Exeunt* PROVOST [*with* CLAUDIO].

DUKE   The hand that hath made you fair hath made you good;
the goodness that is cheap in beauty makes beauty brief in
goodness, but grace, being the soul of your complexion,   180
shall keep the body of it ever fair. The assault that Angelo
hath made to you, fortune hath conveyed to my understanding, and, but that frailty hath examples for his falling,
I should wonder at Angelo. How will you do to content this
substitute, and to save your brother?   185

ISABELLA   I am now going to resolve him: I had rather my
brother die by the law than my son should be unlawfully born.
But, O, how much is the good Duke deceived in Angelo! If
ever he return, and I can speak to him, I will open my lips
in vain, or discover his government.   190

DUKE   That shall not be much amiss, yet, as the matter now
stands, he will avoid your accusation; he made trial of you
only. Therefore fasten your ear on my advising: to the love I
have in doing good a remedy presents itself. I do make myself believe that you may most uprighteously do a poor   195
wronged lady a merited benefit, redeem your brother from
the angry law, do no stain to your own gracious person, and
much please the absent duke, if peradventure he shall ever
return to have hearing of this business.

ISABELLA   Let me hear you speak farther; I have spirit to do   200
anything that appears not foul in the truth of my spirit.

DUKE   Virtue is bold, and goodness never fearful. Have you
not heard speak of Mariana, the sister of Frederick, the
great soldier who miscarried at sea?

ISABELLA   I have heard of the lady, and good words went with   205
her name.

---

168. **fallible**: subject to weakness or making a mistake.
180. **complexion**: behavior.
190. **discover**: expose.
204. **miscarried**: i.e., failed in his expedition.

ness of the benefit defends the deceit from reproof. What
think you of it?

ISABELLA   The image of it gives me content already, and I trust
it will grow to a most prosperous perfection.

DUKE   It lies much in your holding up. Haste you speedily to   250
Angelo; if for this night he entreat you to his bed, give him
promise of satisfaction. I will presently to Saint Luke's;
there, at the moated grange resides this dejected Mariana.
At that place call upon me, and despatch with Angelo, that
it may be quickly.   255

ISABELLA   I thank you for this comfort. Fare you well, good
father.   *Exit.*

Act 3, Scene 2

Enter ELBOW, POMPEY, OFFICERS.

ELBOW   Nay, if there be no remedy for it, but that you will
needs buy and sell men and women like beasts, we shall
have all the world drink brown and white bastard.

DUKE   O heavens, what stuff is here?

POMPEY   'Twas never merry world since, of two usuries, the   5
merriest was put down, and the worser allowed, by order of
law, a furred gown to keep him warm, and furred with fox
and lambskins too, to signify that craft, being richer than
innocency, stands for the facing.

ELBOW   Come your way, sir.—Bless you, good father friar.   10

DUKE   And you, good brother father. What offence hath this
man made you, sir?

ELBOW   Marry, sir, he hath offended the law, and, sir, we take
him to be a thief too, sir, for we have found upon him, sir,
a strange picklock, which we have sent to the deputy.   15

DUKE   Fie, sirrah, a bawd, a wicked bawd!
The evil that thou causest to be done,
That is thy means to live. Do thou but think

---

253. **moated grange:** country house or farm surrounded by a moat (an artificial river designed to repel invaders).
257. **SD:** the Duke remains onstage here.
3.2. Location: a prison in Vienna; although the Folio text does not have a scene division here, it has become standard for editors to introduce one here.
  3. **brown . . . bastard:** sweet wine, with a pun on *illegitimate child of mixed race.*
  5. **usuries:** i.e., businesses depending on the exchange of commodities for money.
  6. **merriest:** i.e., fornication; **worser:** i.e., usury (money lending).
  8. **craft:** deception.
  9. **facing:** inner edge, with a pun on *boasting.*
 10. **father:** old man.
 15. **picklock:** key or device used to pick locks.

POMPEY   Troth, sir, she hath eaten up all her beef, and she is
herself in the tub.

LUCIO   Why, 'tis good. It is the right of it. It must be so. Ever
your fresh whore and your powdered bawd—an unshunned
consequence—it must be so. Art going to prison, Pompey?   55

POMPEY   Yes, 'faith, sir.

LUCIO   Why, 'tis not amiss, Pompey. Farewell: go, say I sent
thee thither. For debt, Pompey? Or how?

ELBOW   For being a bawd, for being a bawd.

LUCIO   Well, then, imprison him. If imprisonment be the due   60
of a bawd, why, 'tis his right. Bawd is he doubtless, and of an-
tiquity, too, bawd-born. Farewell, good Pompey. Commend
me to the prison, Pompey. You will turn good husband now,
Pompey, you will keep the house.

POMPEY   I hope, sir, your good worship will be my bail.   65

LUCIO   No, indeed, will I not, Pompey, it is not the wear. I
will pray, Pompey, to increase your bondage; if you take it
not patiently, why, your mettle is the more. Adieu, trusty
Pompey!—Bless you, friar.

DUKE   And you.   70

LUCIO   Does Bridget paint still, Pompey? Ha?

ELBOW   Come your ways, sir, come.

POMPEY   You will not bail me then, sir?

LUCIO   Then, Pompey, nor now.—What news abroad, friar?
What news?   75

ELBOW [*To* POMPEY]   Come your ways, sir, come.

LUCIO   Go to kennel, Pompey, go.
                              [*Exeunt* ELBOW, POMPEY, *and* OFFICERS.]
What news, friar, of the Duke?

DUKE   I know none. Can you tell me of any?

LUCIO   Some say he is with the Emperor of Russia, other   80
some, he is in Rome. But where is he, think you?

DUKE   I know not where, but wheresoever, I wish him well.

LUCIO   It was a mad fantastical trick of him to steal from the
state and usurp the beggary he was never born to. Lord Angelo dukes it well in his absence: he puts transgression to't.   85

---

51. **eaten . . . beef:** i.e., taken medicine for venereal disease.
52. **tub:** i.e., taken the cure, of sweating in a tub, for venereal disease.
54. **powdered:** heavily made up with powder (and possibly wearing a powdered wig, due to
her loss of hair from venereal disease); **unshunned:** inevitable.
62. **bawd-born:** born of a bawd; born to be a bawd.
66. **wear:** fashion.
68. **mettle:** courage or spirit; **Adieu:** good-bye (French, "to God").
71. **paint:** apply heavy makeup.
83. **mad fantastical:** crazy, impulsive.
84. **usurp:** seize without authority.

LUCIO   Sir, I was an inward of his. A shy fellow was the Duke, and I believe I know the cause of his withdrawing.

DUKE   What, I prithee, might be the cause?

LUCIO   No, pardon, 'tis a secret must be locked within the 120 teeth and the lips. But this I can let you understand: the greater file of the subject held the Duke to be wise.

DUKE   Wise? Why, no question but he was.

LUCIO   A very superficial, ignorant, unweighing fellow.

DUKE   Either this is envy in you, folly, or mistaking. The very 125 stream of his life, and the business he hath helmed, must upon a warranted need give him a better proclamation. Let him be but testimonied in his own bringing-forth, and he shall appear to the envious a scholar, a statesman, and a soldier. Therefore you speak unskilfully, or, if your knowledge be 130 more, it is much darkened in your malice.

LUCIO   Sir, I know him, and I love him.

DUKE   Love talks with better knowledge, and knowledge with dearer love.

LUCIO   Come, sir, I know what I know. 135

DUKE   I can hardly believe that, since you know not what you speak. But, if ever the Duke return—as our prayers are he may—let me desire you to make your answer before him. If it be honest you have spoke, you have courage to maintain it. I am bound to call upon you, and, I pray you, your name? 140

LUCIO   Sir, my name is Lucio, well known to the Duke.

DUKE   He shall know you better, sir, if I may live to report you.

LUCIO   I fear you not.

DUKE   O, you hope the Duke will return no more, or you imagine me too unhurtful an opposite. But, indeed, I can do you 145 little harm. You'll forswear this again?

LUCIO   I'll be hanged first! Thou art deceived in me, friar. But no more of this. Canst thou tell if Claudio die tomorrow or no?

DUKE   Why should he die, sir? 150

LUCIO   Why? For filling a bottle with a tun-dish. I would the Duke we talk of were returned again. This ungenitured agent

---

117. **inward:** confidant.
122. **greater . . . subject:** majority of the Duke's subjects.
124. **unweighing:** i.e., unable to make judgments.
126. **stream:** direction or purpose.
127. **proclamation:** verbal account of his reputation.
128. **testimonied . . . bringing-forth:** made to speak on his own accomplishments.
146. **forswear:** deny.
151. **filling . . . tun-dish:** fornicating (a *tun-dish* is a "funnel").
152. **ungenitured agent:** sexless substitute.

ESCALUS   That fellow is a fellow of much license. Let him be   180
    called before us. Away with her to prison.—Go to, no more
    words.   [*Exeunt* OFFICERS *with* MISTRESS OVERDONE.]
    Provost, my brother Angelo will not be altered, Claudio must
    die tomorrow. Let him be furnished with divines, and have
    all charitable preparation. If my brother wrought by my   185
    pity it should not be so with him.
PROVOST   So please you, this friar hath been with him, and
    advised him for the entertainment of death.
ESCALUS   Good even, good father.
DUKE   Bliss and goodness on you!   190
ESCALUS   Of whence are you?
DUKE   Not of this country, though my chance is now
    To use it for my time: I am a brother
    Of gracious order, late come from the See
    In special business from his holiness.   195
ESCALUS   What news abroad i'th'world?
DUKE   None, but that there is so great a fever on goodness,
    that the dissolution of it must cure it. Novelty is only in re-
    quest, and as it is as dangerous to be aged in any kind of
    course as it is virtuous to be constant in any undertaking.   200
    There is scarce truth enough alive to make societies secure,
    but security enough to make fellowships accurst. Much
    upon this riddle runs the wisdom of the world. This news
    is old enough, yet it is every day's news. I pray you, sir, of
    what disposition was the Duke?   205
ESCALUS   One that, above all other strifes, contended espe-
    cially to know himself.
DUKE   What pleasure was he given to?
ESCALUS   Rather rejoicing to see another merry, than merry
    at anything which professed to make him rejoice: a gentleman   210
    of all temperance. But leave we him to his events, with a
    prayer they may prove prosperous, and let me desire to know
    how you find Claudio prepared. I am made to understand
    that you have lent him visitation.
DUKE   He professes to have received no sinister measure from   215
    his judge, but most willingly humbles himself to the deter-
    mination of justice. Yet had he framed to himself, by the

184. **divines:** spriritual advisers.
185. **brother:** i.e., Angelo.
189. **even:** evening.
194. **gracious order:** high-ranking sect of friars; **See:** i.e., the Vatican.
195. **his holiness:** the pope.
202. **fellowships:** friendships.
211. **temperance:** moderation; **events:** travels or adventures.
215. **sinister:** illegal or unfair.

An 1821 illustration of Act 4, Scene 1, in which the Boy sings to the dejected Mariana.

Act 4, Scene 1

Enter MARIANA *and* [a] BOY *singing*

SONG   Take, O, take those lips away,
   That so sweetly were forsworn,
And those eyes, the break of day,
   Lights that do mislead the morn,

4.1. Location: a moated grange.
  1. **Song**: the first stanza of this song appears (with a second stanza) in a late 1610s King's Men's play, *Rollo, Duke of Normandy, or, The Bloody Brother*; if not written for Shakespeare's play, the song may have been added here sometime after its composition for *Rollo* (or some other play).
  2. **were forsworn**: lied.

The way twice o'er.

DUKE   Are there no other tokens
Between you 'greed concerning her observance?

ISABELLA   No, none, but only a repair i'th'dark;   40
And that I have possessed him my most stay
Can be but brief, for I have made him know
I have a servant comes with me along
That stays upon me, whose persuasion is
I come about my brother.

DUKE   'Tis well borne up.   45
I have not yet made known to Mariana
A word of this.—What ho, within, come forth.

            Enter MARIANA.

I pray you be acquainted with this maid;
She comes to do you good.

ISABELLA   I do desire the like.

DUKE   Do you persuade yourself that I respect you?   50

MARIANA   Good friar, I know you do, and have found it.

DUKE   Take, then, this your companion by the hand,
Who hath a story ready for your ear.
I shall attend your leisure, but make haste:
The vaporous night approaches.   55

MARIANA [*To* ISABELLA]   Will't please you walk aside?
                        [MARIANA *and* ISABELLA *walk aside.*]

DUKE   O place and greatness, millions of false eyes
Are stuck upon thee. Volumes of report
Run with these false and most contrarious quest
Upon thy doings. Thousand escapes of wit   60
Make thee the father of their idle dream,
And rack thee in their fancies. [MARIANA *and* ISABELLA *return.*]
Welcome! How agreed?

ISABELLA   She'll take the enterprise upon her, father,
If you advise it.

DUKE   It is not my consent,   65
But my entreaty too.

ISABELLA   Little have you to say,
When you depart from him, but, soft and low,

39. **'greed:** agreed.
40. **repair:** withdrawal.
55. **vaporous:** foggy or misty.
57. **place and greatness:** i.e., position of power and authority.
58. **report:** verbal comments (including slander).
62. **rack:** distort.
67. **soft and low:** i.e., quietly.

the present and dismiss him. He cannot plead his estimation
with you: he hath been a bawd.

ABHORSON   A bawd, sir? Fie upon him, he will discredit our
mystery.

PROVOST   Go to, sir, you weigh equally: a feather will turn   25
the scale.   *Exit.*

POMPEY   Pray, sir, by your good favor, for, surely, sir, a good favor
you have, but that you have a hanging look. Do you call, sir,
your occupation a mystery?

ABHORSON   Ay, sir, a mystery.   30

POMPEY   Painting, sir, I have heard say, is a mystery, and your
whores, sir, being members of my occupation, using painting,
do prove my occupation a mystery, but what mystery there
should be in hanging, if I should be hanged, I cannot imagine.

ABHORSON   Sir, it is a mystery.   35

POMPEY   Proof?

ABHORSON   Every true man's apparel fits your thief. If it be
too little for your thief, your true man thinks it big enough.
If it be too big for your thief, your thief thinks it little
enough, so every true man's apparel fits your thief.   40

        Enter PROVOST.

PROVOST   Are you agreed?

POMPEY   Sir, I will serve him, for I do find your hangman is
a more penitent trade than your bawd. He doth oftener ask
forgiveness.

PROVOST   You, sirrah, provide your block and your axe to-   45
morrow four o'clock.

ABHORSON   Come on, bawd, I will instruct thee in my trade.
Follow.

POMPEY   I do desire to learn, sir, and I hope, if you have occasion to use me for your own turn, you shall find me yare.   50
For truly, sir, for your kindness, I owe you a good turn.

PROVOST   Call hither Barnardine and Claudio.

                                Exeunt [POMPEY *and* ABHORSON].

One has my pity, not a jot the other,
Being a murderer, though he were my brother.

        21. **estimation:** superior behavior.
        24. **mystery:** professional trade, with a pun on *sacred rite.*
25–26. **you . . . scale:** i.e., Abhorson's profession (executioner) is evenly weighed in shame
        with Pompey's (pimping).
        32. **painting:** applying heavy makeup (to disguise age and blemishes, including those
        caused by venereal disease).
        43. **ask:** ask for.
        45. **block:** executioner's wooden block, on which those being beheaded place their heads.
        50. **yare:** ready.

The steelèd jailer is the friend of men—
  [*Knocking within*]
How now? What noise? That spirit's possessed with haste 80
That wounds th'unsisting postern with these strokes.

   [*Enter* PROVOST.]

PROVOST There he must stay until the officer
Arise to let him in. He is called up.
DUKE Have you no countermand for Claudio yet
But he must die tomorrow?
PROVOST   None, sir, none. 85
DUKE As near the dawning, Provost, as it is,
You shall hear more ere morning.
PROVOST   Happily
You something know, yet I believe there comes
No countermand. No such example have we.
Besides, upon the very siege of justice, 90
Lord Angelo hath to the public ear
Professed the contrary.

   Enter a MESSENGER.

DUKE   This is his lordship's man.
PROVOST And here comes Claudio's pardon.
MESSENGER My lord hath sent you this note, and by me this
  further charge, that you swerve not from the smallest ar- 95
  ticle of it, neither in time, matter, or other circumstance.
  Good morrow, for as I take it, it is almost day.
PROVOST I shall obey him.   [*Exit* MESSENGER.]
DUKE [*Aside*] This is his pardon, purchased by such sin
For which the pardoner himself is in. 100
Hence hath offence his quick celerity,
When it is borne in high authority.
When vice makes mercy, mercy's so extended
That for the fault's love is th'offender friended.
Now, sir, what news? 105
PROVOST I told you: Lord Angelo, belike thinking me remiss
  in mine office, awakens me with this unwonted putting-on,
  methinks strangely, for he hath not used it before.

  79. **steelèd:** steely or fierce.
  81. **th'unsisting postern:** the unlocked door.
  84. **countermand:** order canceling the command for execution.
  91. **public ear:** populace.
  101. **celerity:** speed.
  106. **remiss:** careless or negligent.
  107. **unwonted putting-on:** i.e., unnecessary reminder.

ancient skill beguiles me. But in the boldness of my cunning I will lay myself in hazard. Claudio, whom here you   145
have warrant to execute, is no greater forfeit to the law than
Angelo who hath sentenced him. To make you understand
this in a manifested effect, I crave but four days' respite, for
the which you are to do me both a present and a dangerous
courtesy.   150

PROVOST   Pray, sir, in what?

DUKE   In the delaying death.

PROVOST   Alack, how may I do it? Having the hour limited,
and an express command, under penalty, to deliver his head
in the view of Angelo? I may make my case as Claudio's, to   155
cross this in the smallest.

DUKE   By the vow of mine order, I warrant you, if my instructions may be your guide. Let this Barnardine be this
morning executed, and his head borne to Angelo.

PROVOST   Angelo hath seen them both, and will discover the   160
favor.

DUKE   O, death's a great disguiser, and you may add to it.
Shave the head and tie the beard, and say it was the desire
of the penitent to be so bared before his death. You know
the course is common. If anything fall to you upon this, more   165
than thanks and good fortune, by the saint whom I profess
I will plead against it with my life.

PROVOST   Pardon me, good father, it is against my oath.

DUKE   Were you sworn to the Duke, or to the deputy?

PROVOST   To him and to his substitutes.   170

DUKE   You will think you have made no offence if the Duke
avouch the justice of your dealing?

PROVOST   But what likelihood is in that?

DUKE   Not a resemblance, but a certainty. Yet since I see you
fearful that neither my coat, integrity, nor persuasion can   175
with ease attempt you, I will go further than I meant, to pluck
all fears out of you. Look you, sir, here is the hand and seal
of the Duke. You know the character, I doubt not, and the
signet is not strange to you.

PROVOST   I know them both.   180

---

144. **ancient skill**: i.e., at spiritual advising.
145. **lay . . . hazard**: take a risk.
148. **manifested effect**: demonstration that offers proof.
160–61. **discover the favor**: recognize the face.
172. **avouch**: guarantee.
177. **hand**: handwriting.
179. **signet**: official seal (contained on a ring used to stamp documents).

right the tilter, and brave Master Shoetie the great traveller,
and wild Halfcan that stabbed Pots, and, I think, forty more,   15
all great doers in our trade, and are now "for the Lord's sake."

Enter ABHORSON.

ABHORSON   Sirrah, bring Barnardine hither.
POMPEY   Master Barnardine! You must rise and be hanged,
Master Barnardine!
ABHORSON   What ho, Barnardine!   20
BARNARDINE [*Within*]   A pox o'your throats! Who makes that
noise there? What are you?
POMPEY   Your friends, sir, the hangman. You must be so good,
sir, to rise and be put to death.
BARNARDINE [*Within*]   Away, you rogue, away, I am sleepy.   25
ABHORSON   Tell him he must awake, and that quickly too.
POMPEY   Pray, Master Barnardine, awake till you are exe-
cuted, and sleep afterwards.
ABHORSON   Go in to him, and fetch him out.
POMPEY   He is coming, sir, he is coming, I hear his straw rustle.   30

Enter BARNARDINE.

ABHORSON   Is the ax upon the block, sirrah?
POMPEY   Very ready, sir.
BARNARDINE   How now, Abhorson? What's the news with you?
ABHORSON   Truly, sir, I would desire you to clap into your
prayers, for look you, the warrant's come.   35
BARNARDINE   You rogue, I have been drinking all night, I am
not fitted for't.
POMPEY   O, the better, sir, for he that drinks all night and is
hanged betimes in the morning may sleep the sounder all
the next day.   40

Enter DUKE [*disguised as a friar*].

ABHORSON   Look you, sir, here comes your ghostly father. Do
we jest now, think you?

13–14. **Forthright:** one who handles a lance at a tilt or joust; **tilter:** jouster; **Shoetie:**
shoelace.
15. **Halfcan:** drinker who cannot hold his liquor; **Pots:** pot cleaner in a tavern.
16. **"for . . . sake":** cry of prisoners asking for mercy or charity.
21. **pox:** an epithet or curse, with two meanings: (1) smallpox; (2) venereal disease.
30. **straw rustle:** Prisoners slept on beds of straw.
34. **clap:** hurry.
41. **ghostly father:** spiritual confessor, with a pun on *ghost-like* (mysterious and able to
disappear).

And how shall we continue Claudio,
To save me from the danger that might come
If he were known alive?
DUKE   Let this be done:
Put them in secret holds, both Barnardine and Claudio.   80
Ere twice the sun hath made his journal greeting
To yonder generation, you shall find
Your safety manifested.
PROVOST   I am your free dependent.
DUKE   Quick, dispatch, and send the head to Angelo.   85
                                                    Exit PROVOST.
Now will I write letters to Angelo—
The Provost, he shall bear them—whose contents
Shall witness to him I am near at home,
And that, by great injunctions, I am bound
To enter publicly. Him I'll desire   90
To meet me at the consecrated fount,
A league below the city, and from thence,
By cold gradation and well-balanced form
We shall proceed with Angelo.

                Enter PROVOST [*carrying a head*].

PROVOST   Here is the head, I'll carry it myself.   95
DUKE   Convenient is it. Make a swift return,
For I would commune with you of such things
That want no ear but yours.
PROVOST   I'll make all speed.   *Exit.*
ISABELLA [*Within*]   Peace, ho, be here!
DUKE   The tongue of Isabel. She's come to know   100
If yet her brother's pardon be come hither,
But I will keep her ignorant of her good,
To make her heavenly comforts of despair
When it is least expected.

                Enter ISABELLA.

ISABELLA   Ho, by your leave!   105
DUKE   Good morning to you, fair and gracious daughter.

81. **journal:** daily.
89. **great injunctions:** official orders.
91. **consecrated:** i.e., holy.
92. **league:** a measure of about three miles.
93. **cold gradation:** i.e., walking slowly and deliberately (step by step); **well-balanced form:** i.e., behavior appropriate to a ruler.
98. **want:** need.

Enter LUCIO.

LUCIO   Good even.
Friar, where's the Provost?
DUKE   Not within, sir.
LUCIO   O pretty Isabella, I am pale at mine heart to see thine   145
eyes so red; thou must be patient. I am fain to dine and sup
with water and bran, I dare not for my head fill my belly,
one fruitful meal would set me to't. But they say the Duke
will be here tomorrow. By my troth, Isabel, I loved thy
brother. If the old fantastical duke of dark corners had been   150
at home, he had lived.   [*Exit* ISABELLA.]
DUKE   Sir, the Duke is marvellous little beholding to your reports, but the best is, he lives not in them.
LUCIO   Friar, thou knowest not the Duke so well as I do. He's
a better woodman than thou takest him for.   155
DUKE   Well, you'll answer this one day. Fare ye well.
LUCIO   Nay, tarry, I'll go along with thee, I can tell thee pretty
tales of the duke.
DUKE   You have told me too many of him already, sir, if they
be true; if not true, none were enough.   160
LUCIO   I was once before him for getting a wench with child.
DUKE   Did you such a thing?
LUCIO   Yes, marry, did I, but I was fain to forswear it, they
would else have married me to the rotten medlar.
DUKE   Sir, your company is fairer than honest. Rest you well.   165
LUCIO   By my troth, I'll go with thee to the lane's end. If
bawdy talk offend you, we'll have very little of it. Nay, friar,
I am a kind of burr, I shall stick.   *Exeunt.*

---

146. **fain:** willing to.
147. **with . . . bran:** i.e., austerely, as a form of penance.
148. **fruitful:** luxurious.
150. **fantastical:** extraordinary or inappropriate; **dark corners:** i.e., moving among the
shadows (secretively).
155. **woodman:** lecher.
163. **forswear:** deny.
164. **rotten medlar:** prostitute (*medlar* is a fruit eaten when rotten).
166. **troth:** truth.
168. **burr:** prickly seed or flowerhead that easily becomes imbedded (as in clothing or a shoe).

Act 4, Scene 5

Enter DUKE *[in his own clothes] and* FRIAR PETER.

DUKE *[Giving letters]*   These letters at fit time deliver me.
  The Provost knows our purpose and our plot.
  The matter being afoot, keep your instruction
  And hold you ever to our special drift,
  Though sometimes you do blench from this to that   5
  As cause doth minister. Go, call at Flavius' house,
  And tell him where I stay; give the like notice
  To Valentinus, Rowland, and to Crassus,
  And bid them bring the trumpets to the gate.
  But send me Flavius first.
PETER   It shall be speeded well.   *[Exit.]*   10

Enter VARRIUS.

DUKE   I thank thee, Varrius, thou hast made good haste.
  Come, we will walk. There's other of our friends
  Will greet us here anon, my gentle Varrius.   *Exeunt.*

Act 4, Scene 6

Enter ISABELLA *and* MARIANA.

ISABELLA   To speak so indirectly I am loath;
  I would say the truth, but to accuse him so,
  That is your part, yet I am advised to do it,
  He says, to veil full purpose.
MARIANA   Be ruled by him.
ISABELLA   Besides, he tells me that, if peradventure   5
  He speak against me on the adverse side,
  I should not think it strange, for 'tis a physic
  That's bitter to sweet end.

4.5. Location: a monastery in Vienna.
  3. afoot: i.e., at hand.
  5. blench: flinch.
  9. trumpets: trumpeters heralding the entrance of a ruler.
  13. anon: presently.
4.6. Location: a street in Vienna.
  4. veil: hide.
  5. peradventure: by chance.
  6. adverse: opposing or contradictory.
  7. physic: medicine.

You must walk by us on our other hand,
And good supporters are you.

Enter [FRIAR] PETER *and* ISABELLA.

PETER   Now is your time. Speak loud, and kneel before him.   20
ISABELLA   Justice, O royal Duke! Vail your regard
Upon a wronged—I would fain have said a maid.
O worthy prince, dishonor not your eye
By throwing it on any other object
Till you have heard me in my true complaint,   25
And given me justice, justice, justice, justice!
DUKE   Relate your wrongs. In what? By whom? Be brief:
Here is Lord Angelo shall give you justice.
Reveal yourself to him.
ISABELLA   O worthy duke,
You bid me seek redemption of the devil,   30
Hear me yourself, for that which I must speak
Must either punish me, not being believed,
Or wring redress from you.
Hear me! Oh, hear me here!
ANGELO   My lord, her wits, I fear me, are not firm.   35
She hath been a suitor to me for her brother,
Cut off by course of justice.
ISABELLA   By course of justice!
ANGELO   And she will speak most bitterly and strange.
ISABELLA   Most strange, but yet most truly, will I speak.
That Angelo's forsworn, is it not strange?   40
That Angelo's a murderer, is't not strange?
That Angelo is an adulterous thief,
An hypocrite, a virgin-violator,
Is it not strange? And strange?
DUKE   Nay, it is ten times strange.
ISABELLA   It is not truer he is Angelo   45
Than this is all as true as it is strange:
Nay, it is ten times true, for truth is truth
To th'end of reck'ning.
DUKE   Away with her! Poor soul,
She speaks this in the infirmity of sense.

---

21. **Vail:** lower or cast down.
22. **maid:** (1) young woman, hence unmarried; (2) virgin.
33. **redress:** remedy or appeal.
48. **reck'ning:** reckoning, the Last Judgment (at the end of the world), at which God judges
all the dead.

DUKE   I wish you now, then,
　Pray you take note of it, and when you have
　A business for yourself, pray Heaven you then
　Be perfect.
LUCIO   I warrant your honor.
DUKE   The warrant's for yourself, take heed to't.   85
ISABELLA   This gentleman told somewhat of my tale.
LUCIO   Right.
DUKE   It may be right, but you are i'th'wrong
　To speak before your time.—Proceed.
ISABELLA   I went
　To this pernicious caitiff deputy—   90
DUKE   That's somewhat madly spoken.
ISABELLA   Pardon it,
　The phrase is to the matter.
DUKE   Mended again. The matter: proceed.
ISABELLA   In brief, to set the needless process by,
　How I persuaded, how I prayed, and kneeled,   95
　How he refelled me, and how I replied—
　For this was of much length—the vild conclusion
　I now begin with grief and shame to utter.
　He would not, but by gift of my chaste body
　To his concupiscible intemperate lust,   100
　Release my brother, and, after much debatement,
　My sisterly remorse confutes mine honor,
　And I did yield to him. But the next morn betimes,
　His purpose surfeiting, he sends a warrant
　For my poor brother's head.
DUKE   This is most likely!   105
ISABELLA   O, that it were as like as it is true!
DUKE   By heaven, fond wretch, thou know'st not what thou
　　speak'st,
　Or else thou art suborned against his honor
　In hateful practice. First, his integrity
　Stands without blemish; next, it imports no reason   110

84. **warrant:** assure (the Duke puns on this word in the next line to mean "legal order").
90. **pernicious:** evil.
91. **madly:** insanely.
92. **to the matter:** appropriate to the point being made.
94. **needless process:** i.e., the narration of the full story.
96. **refelled:** refuted.
97. **vild:** vile.
100. **concupiscible intemperate:** lascivious and uncontrollable.
101. **debatement:** debate.
102. **confutes:** overrules.
103. **betimes:** at that point.
108. **suborned:** corrupted.
110. **blemish:** fault; **imports:** demonstrates or carries.

DUKE   We did believe no less.
Know you that Friar Lodowick that she speaks of?   145
PETER   I know him for a man divine and holy,
Not scurvy, nor a temporary meddler,
As he's reported by this gentleman,
And, on my trust, a man that never yet
Did, as he vouches, misreport your grace.   150
LUCIO   My lord, most villainously, believe it.
PETER   Well, he in time may come to clear himself,
But at this instant he is sick, my lord,
Of a strange fever. Upon his mere request,
Being come to knowledge, that there was complaint   155
Intended 'gainst Lord Angelo, came I hither
To speak, as from his mouth, what he doth know
Is true and false, and what he with his oath
And all probation will make up full clear
Whensoever he's convented. First, for this woman,   160
To justify this worthy nobleman,
So vulgarly and personally accused,
Her shall you hear disproved to her eyes,
Till she herself confess it.
DUKE   Good friar, let's hear it.
Do you not smile at this, Lord Angelo?   165
O heaven, the vanity of wretched fools!
Give us some seats. Come, cousin Angelo,
In this I'll be impartial: be you judge
Of your own cause.   [*Exit* OFFICERS *with* ISABELLA.]
Is this the witness, friar?

Enter MARIANA [*veiled*].

First let her show her face, and after speak.   170
MARIANA   Pardon, my lord, I will not show my face
Until my husband bid me.
DUKE   What, are you married?
MARIANA   No, my lord.
DUKE   Are you a maid?
MARIANA   No, my lord.   175
DUKE   A widow, then?

159. **probation:** scrutiny.
160. **convented:** brought here.
167. **Come, cousin Angelo:** the Duke offers his own seat to Angelo here.
169. **SD:** It is not clear when Isabella exits in this scene (the Friar Peter directly refers to her at line 160), but it is most likely here; the Folio text gives her reentrance after line 277; **cause:** legal complaint.
174. **maid:** (1) unmarried woman; (2) virgin.

LUCIO   Carnally, she says!
DUKE   Sirrah, no more.
LUCIO   Enough, my lord.
ANGELO   My lord, I must confess I know this woman,   215
  And five years since there was some speech of marriage
  Betwixt myself and her, which was broke off,
  Partly for that her promised proportions
  Came short of composition, but in chief
  For that her reputation was disvalued   220
  In levity. Since which time of five years
  I never spake with her, saw her, nor heard from her,
  Upon my faith and honor.
MARIANA   Noble prince,
  As there comes light from heaven and words from breath,
  As there is sense in truth and truth in virtue,   225
  I am affianced this man's wife as strongly
  As words could make up vows. And, my good lord,
  But Tuesday night last gone, in's garden-house,
  He knew me as a wife. As this is true,
  Let me in safety raise me from my knees,   230
  Or else for ever be confixèd here,
  A marble monument!
ANGELO   I did but smile till now.
  Now, good my lord, give me the scope of justice,
  My patience here is touched. I do perceive
  These poor informal women are no more   235
  But instruments of some more mightier member
  That sets them on. Let me have way, my lord,
  To find this practice out.
DUKE   Ay, with my heart,
  And punish them to your height of pleasure.
  Thou foolish friar, and thou pernicious woman   240
  Compact with her that's gone. Thinkst thou thy oaths,
  Though they would swear down each particular saint,

---

212. **Carnally:** in the flesh, i.e., sexually, with a pun on the two meanings of *know*, the word
     used by the Duke in line 211, when he asks Angelo if he is acquainted with Isabella, and
     Lucio responds by taking *know* to mean "have sexual experience of"; see note at 5.1.186.
218. **proportions:** i.e., dowry.
219. **composition:** i.e., of the total sum promised.
221. **levity:** lightness, i.e., promiscuity.
228. **in's:** in his.
231. **confixèd:** permanently fixed or stuck.
232. **but smile:** i.e., listened without responding.
234. **touched:** i.e., exhausted.
236. **more mightier member:** higher-ranking conspirator.
240. **pernicious:** evil.
241. **Compact:** conspire.
242. **down:** on.

ESCALUS   I will go darkly to work with her.

LUCIO   That's the way, for women are light at midnight!

ESCALUS [*To* ISABELLA]   Come on, mistress, here's a gentlewoman denies all that you have said.   280

LUCIO   My lord, here comes the rascal I spoke of, here with
the Provost.

ESCALUS   In very good time. Speak not you to him till we call
upon you.

LUCIO   Mum.   285

ESCALUS   Come, sir, did you set these women on to slander
Lord Angelo? They have confessed you did.

DUKE   'Tis false.

ESCALUS   How! Know you where you are?

DUKE   Respect to your great place, and let the devil   290
Be sometime honored for his burning throne!
Where is the Duke? 'Tis he should hear me speak.

ESCALUS   The Duke's in us, and we will hear you speak;
Look you speak justly.

DUKE   Boldly, at least. But Oh, poor souls,   295
Come you to seek the lamb here of the fox?
Good night to your redress! Is the Duke gone?
Then is your cause gone too. The Duke's unjust
Thus to retort your manifest appeal,
And put your trial in the villain's mouth   300
Which here you come to accuse.

LUCIO   This is the rascal, this is he I spoke of.

ESCALUS   Why, thou unreverend and unhallowed friar!
Is't not enough thou hast suborned these women
To accuse this worthy man, but, in foul mouth,   305
And in the witness of his proper ear,
To call him villain, and then to glance from him
To th'duke himself, to tax him with injustice?
Take him hence, to th'rack with him! We'll touze you
Joint by joint, but we will know his purpose.   310

---

277. **darkly:** harshly (Lucio puns in line 278 on this word to mean "in the dark").
278. **light:** promiscuous.
290. **Respect:** i.e., I give respect, used ironically.
291. **burning throne:** the Duke, disguised as a friar, likens the chairs in which Angelo and
Escalus sit to that of the devil because both men appear to be sanctioning evil.
293. **The Duke's in us:** i.e., we represent the Duke.
297. **redress:** remedy.
299. **manifest appeal:** appeal proven to be true.
303. **unreverend** unholy, with a pun on the Friar being a reverend, or clergyman;
unhallowed: unblessed.
304. **suborned:** corrupted.
309. **th'rack:** the rack, an instrument of torture; **touze:** push or shove around.

The Duke (Daniel Massey) judges the penitent Angelo (David Schofield) as Mariana (Emma Watson) and Escalus (Joseph O'Conor) listen in Act 5, Scene 1, of the 1983 Royal Shakespeare Company Production.

Away with those giglots too, and with the other confederate
companion!   345
    [*The* PROVOST *lays hands on the* DUKE.]
DUKE   Stay, sir, stay awhile.
ANGELO   What, resists he? Help him, Lucio.
LUCIO   Come, sir, come, sir, come, sir! Foh, sir! Why, you
bald-pated lying rascal! You must be hooded, must you?
Show your knave's visage, with a pox to you! Show your   350
sheep-biting face, and be hanged an hour! Will't not off?
    [*Pulls off the friar's hood and discovers the* DUKE]
DUKE   Thou art the first knave that e'er made a duke.
First, Provost, let me bail these gentle three.

344. giglots: lewd girls.
350. knave's visage: foolish man's face.
351. sheep-biting: thieving; **an:** in an.
352. knave: foolish or low-born man.

DUKE   You are pardoned, Isabel.
  And now, dear maid, be you as free to us.
  Your brother's death, I know, sits at your heart,   385
  And you may marvel why I obscured myself,
  Laboring to save his life, and would not rather
  Make rash remonstrance of my hidden power
  Than let him so be lost. O most kind maid,
  It was the swift celerity of his death,   390
  Which I did think with slower foot came on,
  That brained my purpose. But peace be with him!
  That life is better life, past fearing death,
  Than that which lives to fear. Make it your comfort,
  So happy is your brother.
ISABELLA   I do, my lord.   395

Enter ANGELO, MARIANA, PETER, *and* PROVOST.

DUKE   For this new-married man approaching here,
  Whose salt imagination yet hath wronged
  Your well-defended honor, you must pardon
  For Mariana's sake. But as he adjudged your brother,
  Being criminal, in double violation   400
  Of sacred chastity and of promise-breach,
  Thereon dependent, for your brother's life,
  The very mercy of the law cries out
  Most audible, even from his proper tongue:
  "An Angelo for Claudio, death for death.   405
  Haste still pays haste, and leisure answers leisure;
  Like doth quit like, and measure still for measure."
  Then, Angelo, thy fault's thus manifested,
  Which, though thou wouldst deny, denies thee vantage.
  We do condemn thee to the very block   410
  Where Claudio stooped to death, and with like haste.—
  Away with him.
MARIANA   O my most gracious lord,
  I hope you will not mock me with a husband?

---

388. **remonstrance:** demonstration.
390. **celerity:** speed.
391. **foot:** speed.
392. **brained:** stifled.
397. **salt:** i.e., lewd.
401. **promise-breach:** breach of promise, i.e., breaking of a legal contract.
407. **measure . . . measure:** alluding to the Bible (Matthew 7:1–2): "Judge not, that ye be not judged. For with what judgment ye judge, ye shall be judged: and with what measure you mete, it shall be measured to you again."
409. **vantage:** advantage.

That perished by the way. Thoughts are no subjects,
Intents but merely thoughts.
MARIANA   Merely, my lord.   450
DUKE   Your suit's unprofitable. Stand up, I say.
I have bethought me of another fault.
Provost, how came it Claudio was beheaded
At an unusual hour?
PROVOST   It was commanded so.
DUKE   Had you a special warrant for the deed?   455
PROVOST   No, my good lord, it was by private message.
DUKE   For which I do discharge you of your office;
Give up your keys.
PROVOST   Pardon me, noble lord:
I thought it was a fault, but knew it not,
Yet did repent me after more advice,   460
For testimony whereof, one in the prison,
That should by private order else have died,
I have reserved alive.
DUKE   What's he?
PROVOST   His name is Barnardine.
DUKE   I would thou hadst done so by Claudio.
Go fetch him hither. Let me look upon him.   465
                                        [*Exit* PROVOST.]
ESCALUS   I am sorry one so learned and so wise
As you, Lord Angelo, have still appeared,
Should slip so grossly, both in the heat of blood
And lack of tempered judgment afterward.
ANGELO   I am sorry that such sorrow I procure,   470
And so deep sticks it in my penitent heart
That I crave death more willingly than mercy.
'Tis my deserving, and I do entreat it.

               Enter PROVOST *with* BARNARDINE *and* CLAUDIO
               [*muffled*], JULIET.

DUKE   Which is that Barnardine?
PROVOST   This, my lord.
DUKE   There was a friar told me of this man.—   475
Sirrah, thou art said to have a stubborn soul
That apprehends no further than this world,
And squar'st thy life according. Thou'rt condemned,

---

448. **no subjects:** i.e., not actions.
450. **Merely:** i.e., just so.
468. **grossly:** obviously; **heat of blood:** passion.
473. **SD *muffled*:** with his head covered with a hood.
478. **squar'st:** accepts.

LUCIO   Marrying a punk, my lord, is pressing to death, whip-
　　ping, and hanging!
DUKE   Slandering a prince deserves it.
　　　　　　　　　　　[*Exeunt* OFFICERS *with* LUCIO.]
　　She, Claudio, that you wronged, look you restore.   520
　　Joy to you, Mariana! Love her, Angelo!
　　I have confessed her, and I know her virtue.
　　Thanks, good friend Escalus, for thy much goodness;
　　There's more behind that is more gratulate.
　　Thanks, Provost, for thy care and secrecy,   525
　　We shall employ thee in a worthier place.
　　Forgive him, Angelo, that brought you home
　　The head of Ragozine for Claudio's;
　　Th'offence pardons itself. Dear Isabel,
　　I have a motion much imports your good,   530
　　Whereto if you'll a willing ear incline,
　　What's mine is yours, and what is yours is mine.
　　So, bring us to our palace, where we'll show
　　What's yet behind that's meet you all should know.   *Exeunt.*

---

517. **punk:** prostitute; **pressing to death:** punishment in which prisoners were crushed to
　　death by heavy stones.
520. **restore:** i.e., restore to honor.
522. **confessed:** acted as her holy confessor.
524. **gratulate:** congratulatory.
530. **motion:** proposal or proposition.
534. **behind:** unexplained.

A Note on the Text

The first recorded performance of *Measure for Measure* was in the banqueting hall of Whitehall Palace on December 26, 1604, but the play was apparently not printed in quarto or other form until 1623, when it appears as the fourth play in the First Folio, where it is listed as a comedy. This text was almost certainly printed from a manuscript of the play copied by Ralph Crane, a professional scribe, who may have been hired to copy out all the plays to be printed in the Folio, but stopped, for some reason, after preparing only the first several to be published there. Crane's transcript shows his characteristic neatness and discipline, especially in making act and scene divisions; regularizing speech prefixes, stage directions, and other formal aspects of the text; and providing at the end of the play a *dramatis personae* (in which he gives the Duke's name as "Vincentio," a name that does not appear anywhere in the text itself, but which may have been supplied by the actors). Crane also hyphenated compound words and routinely inserted apostrophes, colons, and parentheses. He probably also relineated lines that he assumed were "split"—that is, when confronted with a short line at the end of a character's speech, he apparently split the first line of dialogue in the next character's speech so that the two lines would form one pentameter line.

However, Crane's copy also preserves elements of the text from which it was copied, most likely Shakespeare's own "foul papers," or first draft, of the play and not a theatrical transcript or company "book" (used to prompt actors). So, although Crane corrected the formal matter surrounding the dialogue, he did not correct or revise the dialogue itself or the structure or other authorial matter in the play. Crane let stand a number of inconsistencies (as in giving the period of the Duke's laxity in enforcing the laws first as nineteen years in Act 1, Scene 3 and then as fourteen in Act 1, Scene 4) and duplications (in Mistress Overdone announcing Claudio's arrest to Lucio and the two Gentlemen in Act 1, Scene 2 and then seeming to be ignorant of it after Pompey enters a few lines later). All these "false starts" suggest an author in the act of composing, and possibly revising, who has not yet re-copied and corrected his first draft. Other characteristic signs of Shakespeare at work are the generic names of Mistress Overdone (as "Bawd") and Pompey (as "Clown") in speech prefixes and stage acters' names (Mistress Overdone and Pompey) given in the dialogue. Emendations or additions to the stage directions are marked by brackets; however, *Exit* has been emended to *Exeunt* when necessary without the use of brackets. This edition adopts Edward Capell's division of Act 3 (printed in the Folio as one scene) into two scenes, as has become standard in modern editions of the play.

The textual notes that follow record only substantive variants between the Folio text and this edition; in a few instances, this edition has been emended with corrections from the second Folio (1634) or third Folio (1664). Accidental variants in spelling or punctuation (which do not alter the meaning of a word or phrase) are not recorded, nor are changes in lineation (especially from verse to prose or prose to verse). Historical collations are noted only in cases in which an earlier editor's emendation has since become standard for editors.

Textual Variants*

Dramatis Personae] *this edition;* the names of all the Actors *(after "The Scene Vienna." at 5.1.534 in F)* servant to Mistress Overdone] *this edition; not in F*
the scene Vienna] *after 5.1.534 in F*

Act 1, Scene 1] *Actus Primus, Scena Prima F*
10 city's institutions] *this edition; Cities Institutions F*
35 touched] *this edition;* tonch'd *F*
48 metal] *this edition;* mettle *F*
75 *Exit*] *F2; after line 74 in F*

Act 1, Scene 2] *Scena Secunda F*
42 MISTRESS OVERDONE] *this edition; Bawde* (or *Bawd*) *in SD and speech prefixes throughout the play*
80 POMPEY] *this edition; Clowne* (or *Clown*) *in SD and speech prefixes throughout the play.*
80 SD] *this edition; after line 81 in F*

Act 1, Scene 3] *Scena Tertia F*
18 morality] *Rowe;* mortality *F*

Act 1, Scene 4] *Scena Quarta F*

---

*Abbreviations: *F*, Folio 1; *F2*, Folio 2; *F3*, Folio 3; *SD*, stage directions. Editions cited: Rowe (1709), Theobald (1733), Hanmer (1743–44), Warburton (1747), Johnson (1765), Capell (1767–68), and Keightley (1864).

110 PROVOST [*Reads the letter*] *this edition; The Letter. (as centered SD) F*

112 Barnardine] *this edition*; Bernardine *F*

132 reckless] *Pope*; wreaklesse *F*

Act 4, Scene 3] *Scena Tertia F*

13–14 Forthright] *Warburton; Forthlight F*

21 (*Within*)] *this edition*; Barnardine *within. (as centered SD after line 20) F*

82 yonder] *Rowe*; yond *F*

93 well-balanced] *this edition*; weale-ballanc'd *F*

99 *Within*] *this edition*; Isabella *within (as centered SD before this line) F*

Act 4, Scene 4] *Scena Quarta. F*

4 redeliver] *this edition*; reliver *F*

Act 4, Scene 5] *Scena Quinta F*

Act 4, Scene 6] *Scena Sexta F*

4 veil] *this edition*; vaile *F*

Act 5, Scene 1] *Actus Quintus. Scoena Prima F*

14 me] *F3*; we *F*

107 thou] *F3*; yᵘ *F*

170 her] *F2*; your *F*

419 confiscation] *F2*; confutation *F*

534 that's] *F2*; that *F*

SOURCES

Probable Sources

GIRALDI CINTHIO

From Hecatommithi[†]

The Story of Epitia

[Juriste is sent by the Emperor Maximian to Innsbruck where he has a young man arrested and condemned to death for raping a virgin. The young man's sister seeks to free him. Juriste gives her hopes that he will marry her and liberate her brother. She lies with him, and the same night Juriste has the young man's head cut off and sends it to the sister. She complains to the Emperor, who makes Juriste marry her and then gives him up to be executed, but the lady sets him free and lives lovingly with him.]

* * * While this great Lord [Emperor Maximian], who was a rare example of courtesy, magnanimity and singular justice, reigned happily over the Roman Empire, he sent out his ministers to govern the states that flourished under his rule. And among them he sent to govern Innsbruck one of his intimates, a man very dear to him named Juriste. Before sending him he said, 'Juriste, the good opinion I have formed of you while you have been in my service makes me send you as Governor to this noble City of Innsbruck. I could instruct you about many things concerning your rule there but I shall limit myself to one thing only, which is: that you keep Justice inviolate, even if you have to give sentence against me who am your overlord. And I warn you that I could forgive you all other faults, whether you did them through ignorance or through negligence (though I wish you to guard against this as much as possible), but anything done against Justice could never obtain pardon from me.' * * *

---

† From *Hecatommithi* (1583), Decade 8. Novella 5, translated by Geoffrey Bullough (1958) in *Narrative and Dramatic Sources of Shakespeare*, Volume 2: *The Comedies, 1597–1603* (London: Routledge & Kegan Paul; New York: Columbia University Press, 1958), pp. 420–30. For a discussion of all the sources see this volume by Bullough and his article "Another Analogue of *Measure for Measure*," in *English Renaissance Drama: Essays in Honor of Madeleine Doran & Mark Eccles*, edited by S. Henning, R. Kimbrough, and Richard Knowles (Carbondale: Southern Illinois University Press, 1976). pp. 108–17. Reprinted by permission of Columbia University Press and Taylor & Francis Books UK. All notes are by the editor.

they enable me to give your brother his freedom, I shall give him to you the more willingly because I should have been grieved to see him led out to his death through the rigour of the hard law which has imposed it.' * * *

So Epitia departed, full of hope, and went to her brother whom she informed of what she had done with Juriste and how much hope she had obtained from the first interview. In his desperate situation this was very welcome to Vico, and he prayed her to beg for his release. His sister promised to make every effort to that end.

Juriste meanwhile, in whose mind the form of Epitia had deeply impressed itself, turned all this thoughts—lascivious as they became—towards enjoying her, and he waited eagerly for her to come back and speak to him. After three days she returned and asked him courteously what he had decided. He said, 'Welcome lovely maiden; I have not failed to examine diligently all that your arguments could do in your brother's cause, and I have myself searched for others so that you might rest content; but I find that every thing points to his death. For there is a universal law, that when a man sins, not through ignorance, but negligently, his crime cannot be excused, since he ought to know that all men without exception should live virtuously; he who sins in neglect of this principle deserves neither pardon nor pity. Your brother was in his position; he must have been fully aware that anybody who raped a virgin deserved to die; so he must die for it, nor can I reasonably accord him mercy. Nevertheless, for your sake, whom I long to please, if, in your great love for your brother, you are willing to let me enjoy your favours, I am disposed to allow him his life and change the death penalty to one less grave.'

At these words Epitia's cheeks blushed fiery red and she replied: 'My brother's life is very dear to me, but still dearer is my virtue, and I would much sooner try to save him by giving up my life than by losing my honour. Set aside this dishonourable suggestion of yours; but if by other means of pleasing you I can win back my brother I shall do so very gladly.' 'There is no other way,' said Juriste, 'and you should not behave so coyly, for it might easily happen that our first coming-together would result in your becoming my wife.' 'I do not wish,' said Epitia 'to put my honour in danger.' 'But why in danger?' asked Juriste. 'You may well become my wife though now you cannot think it could ever be. Think well upon it, and I shall expect your answer tomorrow.' 'I can give you my answer at once,' she said, 'Unless you take me for your wife, if you really mean that my brother's release depends on that, you are throwing your words to the wind.' Again Juriste replied that she should think it over before returning with her answer, considering who he was, what power he had, and how useful he could be not only to her but to any of her friends, since he had in his hand both Reason and Authority.

Hearing this Epitia went home full of joy, expecting her brother's liberation. The gaoler had Vico's body put on a bier, set the head at its feet, and covering it with a pall had it carried to Epitia, himself going before. Entering the house he called for the young lady, and 'This,' he said, 'is your brother whom my lord Governor sends you freed from prison.' With these words he had the bier uncovered and offered her brother in the way you have heard.

I do not believe that tongue could tell or human mind could comprehend the nature and depth of Epitia's anguish on being thus offered her brother's corpse when she was so joyfully expecting to see him alive and released from all penalties. * * * She, whom Philosophy had taught how the human soul should bear itself in every kind of fortune, showed herself unmoved. She said to the gaoler: 'You will tell your lord—and mine—that I accept my brother in the way in which he has been pleased to send him to me; and although he has not wished to fulfil my desire, I remain content to have fulfilled his; and thus I make his will my own, assuming that what he has done he must have done justly. I send him my respects, offering myself as always ready to do his will.'

The gaoler took back Epitia's message to Juriste, telling him that she had shown no sign of discomposure at so horrible a spectacle. Juriste was happy at this, reflecting that he could have had his will of the maid no more satisfactorily even if she had been his wife and if he had sent her Vico alive.

But Epitia, when the gaoler had departed, fell upon the body of her dead brother, weeping bitterly, complaining long and grievously, cursing Juriste's cruelty and her own simplicity in giving herself to him before he had released her brother. * * * And inciting herself thus to revenge she thought: 'My simplicity opened the way for this soundrel to achieve to the full his dishonest desires. I resolve that his lasciviousness shall give me a way of revenge; and although to seek vengeance will not restore my brother alive, yet it will be a way of removing my vexation of spirit.' And in such a turmoil of ideas her mind closed with the thought that Juriste would send for her to lie with him; going whither she resolved to carry concealed about her a knife and to take the first opportunity she might find of killing him, whether he were awake or asleep; and if she found it possible to cut off his head she would carry it to her brother's tomb and consecrate it to him. But then, thinking it over more maturely she saw that even if she managed to kill the deceiver, it could easily be presumed that she, as a fallen woman and eager therefore for every kind of evil, had done it in an impulse of fury, not because he had failed to keep his word. Then because she had heard how great was the justice of the Emperor (who was then at Villaco) she determined to go and find him and to complain to his Majesty of the ingratitude and injustice shown her by Juriste.

began to beg for mercy, and Epitia on the other hand to demand Justice again.

Realizing the girl's honesty and Juriste's villainy the Emperor deliberated how best to save her honour and preserve Justice, and having resolved in his own mind what he should do, he desired Juriste to marry Epitia. The girl did not want to consent, saying that she could not believe that she would ever receive from him anything but outrages and betrayals. But Maximian insisted that she accept what he had resolved.

Having married Epitia Juriste believed that he had put an end to his woes, but it turned out otherwise, for as soon as Maximian had given the lady leave to return to her inn, he turned to Juriste who had remained there, and said to him, * * * 'Since you have atoned for the first crime by marrying the lady you violated, so in amends for the second I ordain that as you had her brother's head cut off, so shall your own be.' * * * [Juriste] was handed over to the Sergeants to be executed next morning in accordance with the sentence.

* * * Epitia, who had been so ardently against him, when she heard of the Emperor's sentence was moved by her natural benignity and decided it would be unworthy of her, since the Emperor had ordered Juriste to be her husband and she had accepted him, if she consented that he be slain on her account. * * * So, bending all her thoughts to the salvation of the wretched man she went to the Emperor, [saying to him,] 'Most sacred Majesty, let your good intent find its proper end and my honour remain without blemish. I pray you must humbly and reverently, not to ordain by your Majesty's verdict that the sword of Justice cut so woefully the knot with which you have been pleased to tie me to Juriste. Your Majesty's sentence has given clear proof of your Justice; now may it please you, as I sincerely beg, to manifest your Clemency by giving him to me alive. * * * For whereas Justice shows what Vices are hateful and punishes them accordingly, Clemency makes a monarch most like to the immortal Gods.' * * *

It appeared most wonderful to Maximian that she could thrust into oblivion the grave injury she had received from Juriste and pray so warmly for him; and he felt that her generosity merited that he should grant her the life of the wretch who had been so justly condemned to death. So summoning Juriste before him at the very hour when he was expecting to be led out to die, he said to him: 'The generosity of Epitia, you evil man, has such power over my will that although your crime deserves to be punished with a double death, not with one alone, she has moved me to spare your life. Your life, I wish you to understand, comes from her; and since she is willing to live with you, joined in the marriage which I ordained, I am willing to let you live with her. But if I shall ever hear that you treat her as

ACT 5, SCENE 7. CAPTAIN, EMPEROR, EPITIA

CAPTAIN: It seemed to me that if your Majesty
   Had known these things, and had considered too
   The gentle birth of the boy [i.e., Vico], the good 't would do
   To the ravished lady, then indeed you might
   Have tempered the full rigour of the law
   That doomed the hapless Vico to be slain.
   —So I resolved to spare him.
EPITIA: Would you had!
CAPTAIN: And thus intent on saving [Vico] for her,
   I turned my mind this way and that, recalled
   We had in gaol[3] the worst of criminals
   —His tongue already torn out for false witness,
   And now condemned, for murdering his own brother,
   To execution at the very hour
   Of Vico's death. I made them take the head
   Of the murderer—so like Vico in the face
   You'd think it was his own—to the Podestà
   Announcing that the murderer was destroyed
   And Vico was beheaded.

*   *   *

EPITIA: I pray now the cruel cause is moved
   For which he [Juriste] was condemned, he may remain
   In life by your great clemency. I pardon
   Him all offence, and take him for my husband
   Willingly, as your Highness gave him me.

*   *   *

EMPEROR: And even though your brother is not dead
   By prudence of the Captain, yet remains—
   Juriste's aim was death; this evil intent
   Deserves our punishment as if it reached
   The end designed. But that you may be given
   Complete content, I will confer the grace
   You beg, so that, together with your brother,
   Your husband too in life you may enjoy.

3. Jail.

Primary Sources

GEORGE WHETSTONE

From Promos and Cassandra[†]

The Argument of the Whole History

In the Cyttie of *Julio* (sometimes under the dominion of *Corvinus* Kinge of *Hungarie* and *Bohemia*) there was a law, that what man so ever committed Adultery, should lose his head, & the woman offender, should weare some disguised apparel during her life to make her infamouslye noted. This severe law, by the favour of some merciful magistrate, became little regarded, until the time of Lord *Promos* auctority, who convicting a yong Gentleman named *Andrugio* of incontinency, condemned, both him and his minion to the execution of this statute. *Andrugio* had a very vertuous and beautiful Gentlewoman to his Sister, named *Cassandra*. *Cassandra*, to enlarge her brothers life, submitted an humble petition to the Lord *Promos. Promos*, regarding her good behaviours and fantasying her great beauty, was much delighted with the sweete order of her talk; and doing good, that evill might come thereof, for a time, he repry'd her brother, but wicked man, tourning his liking unto unlawfull lust, he set down the spoile of her honour, raunsome for her Brother's life. Chaste *Cassandra*, abhorring both him and his sute,[1] by no perswasion would yeald to this raunsome. But in fine, wonne with the importunitye of her brother (pleading for life) upon these conditions, she agreed to *Promos*: first that he should pardon her brother, and after marry her. *Promos*, as feareles in promisse as careless in performance, with sollemne vowe signed her conditions, but, worse than any Infidel, his will satisfyed, he performed neither the one nor the other; for to keepe his aucthoritye unspotted with favour,

---

† From *The Right Excellent and Famous History of Promos and Cassandra, Divided into Two Comical Discourses* (London: Richard Jones, 1578). For ease of reading this and the following sources, when necessary, *v* has been changed to *u* when used in the primary position, and *u* has been changed to *v* when used in the medial position in a word; thus, for example, *vnkind* has been changed to *unkind*, and *loue* has been changed to *love*. All notes are by the editor.

1. Suit, or plea.

ACT I, SCENE 3. ROSKO (LAMIA's *man*), LAMIA [a courtesan]

ROSKO: Good people, did none of you my mistresse *Lamia* see?
LAMIA: *Rosko*, what newes, that in such haste you come blowing?
ROSKO: Mistresse, you must shut up your shops & leave your
           occupying.
LAMIA: What so they be, foolish knave, tell mee true?
ROSKO: Oh, yll, for thirtie besydes you.
LAMIA: For mee, good fellow, I praye thee why so?
ROSKO: Be patient Mistresse, and you shall knowe.
LAMIA: Go too, saye on.
ROSKO: Marrie, right nowe at the Sessions[7] I was,
           And thirtie must to *Trussum corde* go.[8]
           Among the which (I weepe to showe) alas—
LAMIA: Why, what's the matter man?
ROSKO: O *Andrugio*,
           For loving too kindlie, must loose his heade,
           And his sweete heart must wear the shamefull weedes
           Ordainde for Dames that fall through fleshly deedes.
LAMIA: Is this offence in question come againe?
           Tell, tell no more, 'tys tyme this tale were done:
           See, see howe soone my triumphe turnes to paine. * * *

ACT 2, SCENE I. CASSANDRA, a mayde.[9]

CASSANDRA: Aye, mee, unhappy wenche, that I must live the day,
           To see *Andrugio* tymeless dye, my brother and my stay.
           The onely meane, God wot,[1] that should our house advaunce,
           Who in the hope of his good hap, must dy through wanton chance.

                         *   *   *

           Foule fall thee love, thy lightning joyes hath blasted my welfare.
           Thou fyerst affection fyrst, within my brother's brest.
           Thou mad'st *Polina* graunt him (earst) even what he would request.

                         *   *   *

           The lawe is so severe in scourging fleshly sinne,
           As marriage to worke after mends doth seldome favour win.
           —A law made first of zeale, but wrested much amis.—
           Faults should be measured by desart,[2] but all is one in this.

---

7. Local courts.
8. I.e., hang.
9. Virgin.
1. Know.
2. Deserving.

She kneeling speakes to PROMOS.

Most mighty Lord & worthy Judge, thy judgement sharpe abate,
'Vaile[2] thou thine eares to heare the plaint that wretched I relate;
Behold the wofull Syster here of poore *Andrugio*,
Whom though that lawe awardeth death, yet mercy do him show:
Weigh his yong yeares, the force of love, which forced his amis;[3]
Weigh, Weigh, that Mariage works amends for what committed is.
He hath defilde no nuptial bed, nor forced rape hath mov'd,
He fel through love, who never meant but wive the wight[4] he lov'd.
And wantons sure, to keepe in awe of these statutes first were made,
Or none but lustful lechers should with rygorous law be paid.
And yet to add intent thereto, is far from my pretence,
I sue with teares to win him grace, that sorrows his offence.
Wherefore herein, renowned Lorde, Justice with pitie payse:[5]
Which two in equal ballance waide[6] to heaven your fame will raise.

PROMOS: *Cassandra*, leave of[f] thy bootlesse[7] sute, by law he hath been tride,

Lawe founde his faulte, Lawe judgde him death:

CASSANDRA: Yet this maye be replide,
  That law a mischiefe oft permits, to keepe due forme of lawe,
  That lawe small faults with greatest doomes, to keepe men styl in awe:
  Yet Kings, or such as execute regall authoritie,
  If mends[8] be made may over rule the force of lawe with mercie.
  Here is no wylful murder wrought, which axeth blood againe;
  Andrugios fault may valued be, Mariage wipes out his stayne.

PROMOS: Faire Dame, I see the naturall zeale thou bearest to *Andrugio*,
  And for thy sake (not his desart) this favour will I showe:
  I wyll reprieve him yet a whyle, and on the matter pawse;
  To morrowe you shall lycence have, afresh to pleade his cause:
  Sh[e]reief execute my chardge, but staye *Andrugio*,
  Untill that you in this behalfe more of my pleasure knowe.

SHERIFF: I wyll performe your will:

CASSANDRA: O most worthy Magistrate, my selfe thy thrall I finde,
  Even for this lytle lightning hope which at thy handes I finde.
  Now wyl I go and comfort him, which hangs twixt death & life.   *Exit*

2. Lower.
3. Misdeed.
4. I.e., marry the person.
5. Balance.
6. Weighed.
7. Useless.
8. Amends.

PROMOS: Bethink yourself, at price enough I purchase sweet your
      love,
      Andrugios life suffis'd alone your straungenes to remove:
      The which I graunt, with any wealth that else you wyll require.
      Who buyeth love at such a rate payes well for his desire.
CASSANDRA: No *Promos*, no, honor never at value maye be solde,
      Honor farre dearer is then life, which passeth price of gold.
PROMOS: To buye this Juell at the full, my wife I may thee make.
CASSANDRA: For unsure hope, that peereles pearle I never will
      forsake.

✻   ✻   ✻

PROMOS: I wyll two daies hope styll of thy consent,
      Which if thou graunt (to cleare my clowdes of care)
      Cloth'd like a Page (suspect for to prevent,)
      Unto my Court, some night, sweet wench repaire.
      Till then adue;[4] thou these my words in works perform'd shalt find.
CASSANDRA: Farewel my lord, but in this sute you bootles wast
      your wind.[5]

Exit Promos

      O most unhappy, subject to everie woe,
      What tongue can tel, what thought conceive, what pen they griefe
      can show? ✻ ✻ ✻

ACT 3, SCENE 4. ANDRUGIO *out of prison*,
CASSANDRA *on the stage.*

ANDRUGIO: My *Cassandra*, what newes? Good sister, showe!
CASSANDRA: All thinges conclude thy death, *Andrugio*:
      Prepare thy selfe, to hope it were in vaine.

✻   ✻   ✻

      If thou doest live I must my honor lose.

✻   ✻   ✻

ANDRUGIO: And may it be, a Judge of his account
      Can spot his minde with lawles love or lust?
      But more, may he doome any fault with death
      When in such fau[l]te he findes himselfe injust?

✻   ✻   ✻

      Nay, *Cassandra*, if thou thy selfe submyt,
      To save my life, to *Promos'* fleashly wyll,

---

4. Adieu, or farewell.
5. Waste your breath.

ACT 4, SCENE 2, PROMOS *alone*.

* * *

PROMOS: To pardon him that dyd commit a Rape,
To set him free, I to *Cassandra* sware:
But no man else is privie to the same,
And rage of Love for thousande oathes nyll spare
More then are kept when gotten is the game.
Well, what I sayde, then Lover-like I sayde:
Nowe reason sayes, unto thy credite looke:
And having well the circumstaunces wayde,
I finde I must unsweare the oathe I tooke.
But double wrong I so should do *Cassandra*.
No force for that, my might commaundeth right;
Or if not so, my frowning will hir fright,
And thus shall rule conceale my filthy deede.
Nowe foorthwith I wyll to the Gayler sende
That secretlie *Andrugio* he behead,
Whose head he shall with these same wordes commend:—
To *Cassandra*: as *Promos* promist thee,
From prison, loe, he sendes thy Brother free.

ACT 4, SCENE 3. CASSANDRA.

CASSANDRA: Fayne would I, wretch, conceale the spoyle of my virginity,
But O my g[u]ilt doth make mee blush, chast virgins here to see:
I monster now, no mayde, nor wife, have stoopte to *Promos*' lust.

* * *

O cruell death, nay hell to her that was constrynd to shame! * * *

ACT 4, SCENE 4. GAYLAR, *with a dead man's head
in a charger,*[1] CASSANDRA.

* * *

JAILER: Fayre *Cassandra*, my Lord *Promos* commends me him unto thee
To keepe his word, who sayes from prison he sends thy brother free.
CASSANDRA: Is my *Andrugio* done to death? fye, fye, O faythles trust!

1. Platter.

No force for that, who others doth deceyve,
Deserves himself lyke measure to receyve. * * *

The Second Part of Promos and Cassandra

ACT 3, SCENE 3. Enter the KING, PROMOS [and others]

* * *

[*Enter*] CASSANDRA in *a* blewe gowne, shadowed with
black.

CASSANDRA: O would that teares myght tell my tale, I shame so
much my fall,
Or else, Lord *Promos'* lewdnes showen, would death would ende
my thrall.
PROMOS: Welcome my sweete *Cassandra*.
CASSANDRA: Murdrous varlet, away.
Renowmed King, I pardon crave for this my bould attempt,
In preasing[8] thus so near your grace, my sorrow to present,
And lest my foe, false *Promos* heere, doe interrupt my tale,
Grant gratious King, that uncontrould I may report my bale.[9]
KING: How now *Promos*? How lyke you of this song?
Say on fayre dame, I long to heare thy wrong.
CASSANDRA: Then knowe dread soverayne, that he this doome did
geve,
That my Brother for wantonnesse should lose his head:
And that the mayde which sin'd, should ever after lyve
In some religious house, to sorrowe her misdeede.

* * *

He crav'd this raunsom, to have my virginitie:
No teares could work restryint, his wicked lust was such.
Two evils here were, one must I chuse, though bad were very best,
To see my brother put to death or graunt his lewde request:
In fyne, subdude with naturall love I did agree,
Upon these two poyntes: that marry mee he should,
And that from prison vyle he should my brother free.
All this with monstrous othes he promised he would.
But O this perjurd *Promos*, when he had wrought his wyll,
Fyrst caste me of[f] and after causd the Gailer to kill
My brother, raunsomde with the spoyle of my good name:

---

8. Pressing.
9. Baleful or sorrowful story.

PROMOS: This mone[6] good wife, for Chrysts sake forsake:
I, late resolv'd, through feare of death, now quake.
Not so much for my haynous sinnes forepast,
As for the greefe that present thou dost tast[e].

CASSANDRA: Nay, I vile wretch, should most agreeved be,
Before thy time thy death which hastened have:
But (O swete husband) my fault forgeve mee,
And for amends Ile helpe to fyll thy grave. * * *

They all depart, save POLINA, CASSANDRA, and her woman.

* * *

Enter GANIO sometime ANDRUGIOS Boye

GANIO: O sweete newes for *Polina* and *Cassandra*:
Andrugio lyves.

POLINA: What doth poore *Ganio* saye?

GANIO: *Andrugio* lyves, and *Promos* is repriv'd.

CASSANDRA: Vaine is thy hope, I sawe *Andrugio* dead.

GANIO: Well, then, from death he is againe revyv'd.
Even nowe I sawe him in the market stead.

POLINA: His words are straunge.

CASSANDRA: Too sweete, God wot,[7] for true.

GANIO: I praye you, who are these here in your view?

CASSANDRA: The King.

GANIO: Who more?

POLINA: O, I see *Andrugio*.

CASSANDRA: And I my Lord *Promos*; adue[8] sorrowe!

Enter the KING, ANDRUGIO, PROMOS, ULRICO, the
MARSHALL

POLINA: My good *Andrugio*!
ANDRUGIO: My sweet *Polina*.
CASSANDRA: Lives *Andrugio*? Welcome sweet brother.
ANDRUGIO: *Cassandra*!
CASSANDRA: I.
ANDRUGIO: Howe fare, my deare Syster?

* * *

CASSANDRA: Most gratious King, with these my joye to match,
Vouchsafe to geve my dampned husbande lyfe.

KING: If I doo so, let him thanke thee, his Wife.

6. Moaning.
7. Knows.
8. Adieu, or farewell.

Feare no uproares for doing of justice, since yee may assure your selfe, the most part of your people will ever naturally favour justice: providing always, that ye doe it onely for love to justice, and not for satisfying any particular passions of yours, under colour thereof: otherwise, how justly that ever the offender deserve it, yee are guiltie of murther before God. For ye must consider, that God ever looketh to your inward intention in all your actions.

And when ye have by the severity of justice once settled your counties, and made them knowe that yee can strike, then may yee thereafter all the dayes of your life mixe justice with mercie; punishing or sparing, as ye shall find the crime to have beene wilfullie or rashlie committed, and according to the by-past behaviour of the committer. For if otherwise yee kyth[1] your clemencie at the first, the offences would soone come to such heapes, and the contempt of you growe so great, that when yee would fall to punish, the number of them to be punished would exceed the innocent; and ye would be troubled to resolve whom-at to begin: and against your nature would bee compelled then to wracke many, whome the chastisement of few in the beginning might have preserved. * * *

As this severe justice of yours upon all offences would be but for a time, (as I have already sayd) so is there some horrible crimes that yee are bound in conscience never to forgive: such as Witch-craft, wilfull murther, Incest (especially within the degrees of consanguinitie) Sodomy, Poysoning, and false coyne. As for offences against your owne person and authority, since the fault concerneth your selfe, I remit to your owne choyse to punish or pardon therein, as your heart serveth you, and according to the circumstances of the turne and the qualitie of the committer. * * *

Cherish no man more than a good Pastor, hate no man more than a proude Puritan. * * *

Consider, that mariage is the greatest earthly felicitie or miserie, that can come to a man, according, as it pleaseth God to blesse or curse the same. Since then without the blessing of GOD, yee can not looke for a happie successe in mariage; ye must be carefull both in your preparation for it, and in the choyse and usage of your Wife, to procure the same. By your preparation, I meane, that yee must keepe your bodie cleane and unpolluted, til ye give it to your wife; whome-to onely it belongeth. For how can yee justly crave to bee joined with a pure Virgin, if your bodie be polluted? Why should the one halfe bee cleane, and the other defiled? And although I knowe, Fornication is thought but a light and veniall sine, by the most part of the world; yet remember well what I said to you in my first booke

---

1. Make known.

Analogues

THOMAS LUPTON

From The Second Part of Too Good to Be True†

A notorious example of a detestable Judge

SIUQILA: There was a very yong man, not very far from the
Countrie where I was borne, who for his great learning, rare wise-
dom, commendable conditions, and modest maners, was, by the
Magistrates and Rulers of that Countrie, chosen to be a Judge,
who used him selfe for a while in his Office, so uprightly and so
godlie, to the judgement of every one, that none but were glad
that they had suche a Judge. In whose time, there happened two
Gentlemen to be very conversant together, and to love one another
dearly, even as though they had been sworn brethren: and whiles
they were in friendshippe, the one of them began to cast his love
on a certaine Gentlewoman; who being a great suter¹ unto hir,
and yet could not obtain her love as he wisht began to languish for
hir love.

   [The Gentleman eventually marries the Gentlewoman, although
his friend had attempted to woo her for himself. Later, the Gentleman slays the friend and is imprisoned. The wife appeals to the
Judge.] She kneeled unto him, and with weeping teares saide, O
worthie Judge, as you are counted a most wise and mercifull
Judge, now shew that in effect which is bru[i]ted of you in talke:
and save an Innocents life that lieth in your hands to destroy. To
whom the Judge said: Stand up Gentlewoman; it will greeve me to
see you stand, much more to kneele: therefore without any more
bidding sit downe by me, and I will not onely heare you, but also
helpe you if I be able. * * * [She said:] I am the wife of suche a
Gentleman that killed a man of late, whose cause I come not to
defend, but whom I come to crave mercy. * * *

† From *The Second Part and Knitting Up of the Book Entitled Too Good to Be True* (London,
Henry Binneman, 1581). All notes are by the editor.
1. Suitor.

saide the Judge, he would the more love you, that did that for the saving of his life, which you preferde before your owne life. * * *

If you perform this my demaund nowe, I will save his life; but if you refuse it, then, though you wo[u]ld, I will not: wherefore, now you may save your husbandes life, or within these two or three dayes be moste sure of his death. To whom the Gentlewoman saide, preferring hir husbandes life before all other things in the worlde): Well, sir, seeing there is no remedie, I doe yeelde unto you. * * * I will be here at your privie dore to morrow at night, when I will not only bring you al your gold, but also (though sore against my minde) will performe the rest of my promise. * * *

The Gentlewoman brought the gold at hir houre, by such privie means as she thought convenient, and the Judge received both it and hir, being then something darke, and so she did lie there al the night with the Judge: to whom he said in the morning * * * your husband should have bin executed tomorrow in the morning, I will dispatch him, and send him home tomorrow unto you before noone at the furthest. * * * And thus she departed from the Judge, very merie for the saving of her husbands life, but yet somewhat sorrowful for the breaking of hir faith to hir husband. * * *

The next morning about 8 or 9 of the clocke, this sorrowful Gentlewomans husband was put to death: which, after it was done, was ryfe in every mans mouthe. And the saide Gentlewoman standing at hir dore, saw one come running in all the haste, who seeing him coming toward hir so fast, was very glad, thinking that he came to tel hir of her husbands life: but it fell out otherwayes, for he came to tel hir of her husbands death. * * * With that the good Gentlewoman fel sodainely to the ground. * * *

As speedily as she coulde, she got hir decent mourning attyre, and with convenient men to waite on hir, rode in all the haste where the Magistrates and the chiefe Rulers of the Countery did sit: who knocking at the Counsel Chamber dore, within a while after was lette in, when they knewe who she was. And when she came before them, she kneeled downe: and lamentably and pitifully desired them that she might have Justice, for that was the onely thing she craved: and as all my sute of late (saide she) was chiefly for Mercie, now at my request is onely for Justice. Then saide the chiefe of the Counsell: Gentlewoman, we may perceive that some great matter hath driven you hither to require Justice, therefore tell us your matter truly, and you shall be sure of Justice, and that with all expedition. Then she humbly thanked him, and told in every point and hidde nothing, howe the wicked Judge did use hir.

[The Judge is imprisoned and the Magistrates] agreed that hir honesty could not be saved nor the infamous talke suppressed of hir lying with the Judge, but onely by marrying of the same Judge: and

BARNABY RICH

From The Adventures of Brusanus†

Dorestus Prince of Epirus, to Brusanus, the professed enemy to love and beauty.

[*Brusanus* traveled] towards *Epirus*, wher *Leonarchus* then reigned kinge, a prince that was renowned for his vertue, fortunate for his peacable government, reverenced for his gravity, obayed for his authoritie, loved for his mediocrity, and honoured for his liberalitie, administering justice with such sinceritie, yet tempering the extremitie of the lawe with such limmite, as he gained the good wil of strangers in hearing his vertue and wonne the heartes of his subjectes in feeling his bountie. * * * This noble prince upon a private conceipt to him selfe, disguised in the habit of a marchant, had secretly left his courte, and travelling through many partes of his owne dominions, (being not otherwise taken then for a marchant) called him selfe by the name of *Corynus*. * * *

[*Brusanus* and *Corynus* met] Senior *Gloriosus*, the loftiness of his lookes was much to bee marveld at, but the manner of his attire was more to be laughed at. On his head he wore a hatte without a band like a *Mallcontent*, his haire hanging downe to both his shoulders, as they use to figure a hagge of hell, his beard cut *peecke a devaunt*, turnde uppe a little, like the vice[1] of a play, his countenance strained as far as it would stretch, like a great *Monarcho*; his coller turnde downe round about his necke, that his throat might be seene, as one that were going to a hanging should make way for the hallter, his doublet bolstered with bumbast,[2] as if he had been diseased with the dropsie; uppon that hee wore a loose *Mandilyon*, like a counterfait souldiour, in his hande a fanne of fethers, like a demye-harlot. Riding thus along by them, casting his eies to and fro, seming by his demenure,[3] as if he had had a whole common wealth in his head, without any speaking.

[After the arrest of *Corynus* and others due to false accusations of treason by *Gloriosus*, *Brusanus* goes to hear Prince *Dorestus*, son of *Leonarchus*, speak:] Magistrates in the execution of justice ought to take great heede lest by overgreat severity, they hurt more than they heale. * * * It is the duety of all magistrates to chastise and to punish

---

† From *The Adventures of Brusanus, Prince of Hungaria* (London: Thomas Adams, 1592), Part I, Chapters 5–20. All notes are by the editor.
1. I.e., like the stock character of Vice.
2. Cotton stuffing.
3. Demeanor.

CRITICISM

ALEXANDER POPE

From Preface to *The Works of Shakespear*†

* * * Nor does he only excel in the Passions: In the coolness of Reflection and Reasoning he is full as admirable. His *Sentiments* are not only in general the most pertinent and judicious upon every subject; but by a talent very peculiar, something between Penetration and Felicity, he hits upon that particular point on which the bent of each argument turns, or the force of each motive depends. This is perfectly amazing, from a man of no education or experience in those great and public scenes of life which are usually the subject of his thoughts: So what he seems to have known the world by Intuition, to have look'd thro' humane nature at one glance, and to be the only Author that gives ground for a very new opinion, That the Philosopher and even the Man of the world, may be *Born*, as well as the Poet.

It must be own'd that with all these great excellencies, he has almost as great defects; and that as he has certainly written better, so he has perhaps written worse, than any other. But I think I can in some measure account for these defects, from several causes and accidents; without which it is hard to image that so large and so enlighten'd a mind could ever have been susceptible of them. That all these Continencies should unite to his disadvantage seems to me almost as singularly unlucky, as that so many various (nay contrary) Talents should meet in one man, was happy and extraordinary.

It must be allowed that Stage-Poetry of all other, is more particularly levell'd to please the *Populace*, and its success more immediately depending upon the Common Suffrage. One cannot therefore wonder, if Shakespear having at his first appearance no other aim in his writings than to procure a substance, directed his endeavours solely to hit the taste and humour that then prevailed. The Audience was generally composed of the meaner sort of people: and therefore the Images of Life were to be drawn from those of their own rank: accordingly we find, that not our Author's only but almost all the old Comedies have their Scene among *Tradesmen* and *Mechanicks*.[1] * * * In Comedy, nothing was so sure to *please*, as mean buffonry, vile ribaldry, and unmannerly jests of fools and clowns.

---

† From Preface to *The Works of Shakespear in Six Volumes* (London: Jacob Tonson, 1725), 1:iv–v. All notes are by the editor.

1. I.e., laborers.

properly the Subject of Tragedy, the Design of which is to shew the fatal Consequences of those Crimes, and the Punishment that never fails to attend them. The light Follies of a *Lucio*, may be exposed, ridiculed and corrected in Comedy.

That *Shakespear* made a wrong Choice of his Subject, since he was resolved to torture it into a Comedy, appears by the low Contrivance, absurd Intrigue, and improbable Incidents, he was obliged to introduce, in order to bring about three or four Weddings, instead of one good Beheading, which was the Consequence naturally expected.

The Duke, who it must be confess'd, has an excellent plotting Brain, gives it out that he is going *incognito* to *Poland*, upon weighty Affairs of State, and substitutes *Angelo* to govern till his Return; to Friar *Thomas* his Confidant, however he imparts his true Design, which is, in his Absence, to have some severe Laws revived, that had been long disused: Methinks this Conduct is very unworthy of a good Prince; if he thought it fit and necessary to revive those Laws, why does he commit that to another, which it was his Duty to perform?

* * * It must be confessed indeed, that *Angelo* is a very extraordinary Hypocrite, and thinks in a Manner quite contrary from all others of his Order; for they, as it is natural, are more concerned for the Consequences of their Crimes, than the Crimes themselves, whereas he is only troubled about the Crime, and wholly regardless of the Consequences.

The Character of *Isabella* in the Play seems to be an Improvement upon that of *Epitia* in the Novel; for *Isabella* absolutely refutes, and persists in her Refusal, to give up her Honour to save her Brother's Life; whereas *Epitia*, overcome by her own Tenderness of Nature, and the affecting Prayers of the unhappy Youth, yields to what her Soul abhors, to redeem him from a shameful Death. It is certain however, that *Isabella* is a mere Vixen in her Virtue; how she rates her wretched Brother, who gently urges her to save him! * * *

This Play therefore being absolutely defective in a due Distribution of Rewards and Punishments; *Measure for Measure* ought not to be the Title, since Justice is not the Virtue it inculcates; nor can *Shakespear*'s Invention in the Fable be praised; for what he has altered from Cinthio, is altered greatly for the worse.

Shakespeare with his excellencies has likewise faults, and faults sufficient to obscure and overwhelm any other merit. * * * His first defect is that to which may be imputed most of the evil in books or in men. He sacrifices virtue to convenience, and is so much more careful to please than to instruct, that he seems to write without any moral purpose. From his writings indeed a system of social duty may be selected, for he that thinks reasonably must think morally; but his precepts and axioms drop casually from him; he makes no just distribution of good or evil, nor is always careful to shew in the virtuous a disapprobation of the wicked; he carries his persons indifferently through right and wrong, and at the close dismisses them without further care, and leaves their examples to operate by chance. This fault the barbarity of his age cannot extenuate; for it is always a writer's duty to make the world better, and justice is a virtue independant on time or place. * * *

There is perhaps not one of *Shakespear*'s plays more darkened than this by the peculiarities of its Authour, and the unskilfulness of its Editors, by distortions of phrase, or negligence of transcription. * * *

Of this play the light or comick part is very natural and pleasing, but the grave scenes, if a few passages be excepted, have more labour than elegance. The plot is rather intricate than artful. The time of the action is indefinite; some time, we know not how much, must have elapsed between the recess of the *Duke* and the imprisonment of *Claudio*; for he must have learned the story of Mariana in his disguise, or he delegated his power to a man already known to be corrupted. The unities of action and place are sufficiently preserved.

ELIZABETH INCHBALD

From Remarks on *Measure for Measure*†

Shakspeare displays such genius in the characters, poetry and incident of his dramas, that it is to be regretted, he ever found materials for a plot, excepting those of history, from any other source than his own invention. Had the plots of old tales been exhausted in his time, as in the present, the world might have had Shakspeare's foundation as well as superstructure, and the whole edifice had been additionally magnificent.

"Measure for Measure," like his other plays, is taken from an old story—Cinthio's novels, or a play of Whetstone's, has furnished the

---

† From "Remarks on *Measure for Measure*," in *The British Theatre; or a Collection of Plays, Which Are Acted at the Theatres Royal, Drury Lane, Covent Garden, and Haymarket* (London: Longman, Hurst, Rees & Orme, 1808), 3:sig. B2–B3.

on this play, should write in praise of the comick characters, seems surprising! To a delicate critic of the present day, and one thoroughly acquainted with his moral character, it must surely appear, as if Johnson's pure mind had been somewhat sullied by having merely read them.

WILLIAM HAZLITT

From Characters of Shakespear's Plays†

* * * This is a play as full of genius as it is of wisdom. Yet there is an original sin in the nature of the subject, which prevents us from taking a cordial interest in it. "The height of moral argument" which the author has maintained in the intervals of passion or blended with the more powerful impulses of nature, is hardly surpassed in any of his plays. But there is in general a want of passion; the affections are at a stand; our sympathies are repulsed and defeated in all directions. The only passion which influences the story is that of Angelo; and yet he seems to have a much greater passion for hypocrisy than for his mistress. Neither are we greatly enamoured of Isabella's rigid chastity, though she could not act otherwise than she did. We do not feel the same confidence in the virtue that is "sublimely good" at another's expense, as if it had been put to some less disinterested trial. As to the Duke, who makes a very imposing and mysterious stage-character, he is more absorbed in his own plots and gravity than anxious for the welfare of the state; more tenacious of his own character than attentive to the feelings and apprehensions of others. Claudio is the only person who feels naturally; and yet he is placed in circumstances of distress which almost preclude the wish for his deliverance. Mariana is also in love with Angelo, whom we hate. In this respect, there may be said to be a general system of cross-purposes between the feelings of the different characters and the sympathy of the reader or the audience. This principle of repugnance seems to have reached its height in the character of Master Barnardine, who not only sets at defiance the opinions of others, but has even thrown off all self-regard,—"one that apprehends death no more dreadfully but as a drunken sleep; careless, reckless, and fearless of what's past, present and to come." He is a fine antithesis to the morality and the hypocrisy of the other characters of the play. * * *

We do not understand why the philosophical German critic, Schlegel, should be so severe on those pleasant persons, Lucio, Pompey,

† From *Characters of Shakespear's Plays* (London: C. H. Reynell, 1817), pp. 320–23.

The comic and tragic parts equally border on the *miseton*[1]—the one being disgusting, the other horrible; and the pardon and marriage of Angelo not merely baffles the strong indignant claim of justice—(for cruelty, with lust and damnable baseness, cannot be forgiven, because we cannot conceive them as being morally repented of;) but it is likewise degrading to the character of woman. Beaumont and Fletcher, who can follow Shakspeare in his errors only, have presented a still worse, because more loathsome and contradictory, instance of the same kind in the Night-Walker, in the marriage of Alathe to Algripe. Of the counterbalancing beauties of Measure for Measure, I need say nothing; for I have already remarked that the play is Shakespeare's throughout.

FREDERICK S. BOAS

"The Problem-Plays" and *Measure for Measure*[†]

The opening of the seventeenth century coincides almost exactly with a sharp turning-point in Shakspere's dramatic career. On one side of the year 1601 lie comedies of matchless charm and radiance, and histories which are half comedies. On the other appear plays, in which historical matter is given a tragic setting, or in which comedy for the most part takes the grim form of dramatic satire. The change has been compared to the passage from a sunny charming landscape to a wild mountain-district whose highest peaks are shrouded in thick mist. The causes of this startling alteration in the poet's mood are, as has been shown, in great measure obscure. He was in the full tide of outward prosperity, and though his father died in 1601, this event could not have brought a keener pang than the loss of his only son in 1596, which seems to have left no shadow on his work. The Sonnets, with their record of mental anguish and disillusion, give a partial clue, but it must be acknowledged that the evidences of date tend to place the estrangement between Shakspere and Will during the period of the brightest comedies, and their reconciliation just before the production of the graver plays. Another cause that has been suggested for the dramatist's change from gaiety to gloom, is the failure of the conspiracy of Essex followed by the execution of the Earl and the imprisonment of Shakspere's friend Southampton. To this we might find a parallel in Spenser's *Complaints*, whose pessimistic tone is largely due to his grief at the death of Sidney and Leicester. It can scarcely be a

---

1. Hateful (Greek).
† From *Shakspere and His Predecessors* (London: John Murray, 1896), pp. 344–45, 357–59. All notes are by the editor.

the deepest issues of life here and beyond the grave, that give the play a massive weight which the original framework of plot might well have seemed too slight to bear. * * *

Measure for Measure has never won the suffrages[2] of the majority of readers, and has been condemned by a number of critics, including Coleridge, who calls it 'the most painful—say, rather, the only painful—part' of Shakspere's genuine works, and who speaks of the comic scenes as disgusting, the tragic as horrible. Such criticism, besides entirely passing over the wonderful technical skill which has smoothed away most of the difficulties in peculiarly stubborn materials, is grossly unjust to the spirit of the play. Such epithets as 'disgusting' and 'horrible' can only be fairly applied to scenes which violate aesthetic decencies from sheer love of the foul or the barbarous. In *Measure for Measure*, though undeniably strong meat is served up, the most repulsive details have all their place in the general scheme, which is indisputably noble, while numberless lustrous shafts of poetry and thought pierce the sombre atmosphere in which the action moves.

A. C. BRADLEY

From Shakespearean Tragedy[†]

* * * If he did not succeed at once—and how can even he have always done so?—he returned to the matter again and again. Such things as the scenes of Duncan's murder or Othello's temptation, such speeches as those of the Duke to Claudio and of Claudio to his sister about death, were not composed in an hour and tossed aside; and if they have defects, they have not what Shakespeare thought defects. Nor is it possible that his astonishingly individual conceptions of character can have been struck out at a heat: prolonged and repeated thought must have gone to them. * * *

In those parts of his plays which show him neither in his most intense nor in his most negligent mood, we are often unable to decide whether it was quite decidedly meant to be as it is, and has an intention which we ought to be able to divine; whether, for example, we have before us an unusual trait in character or an abnormal movement of mind, only surprising to us because we understand so very much less of human nature than Shakespeare did, or whether he wanted to get his work done and made a slip, or in following an old play carelessly adopted something that would not square with his own conception, or

---

2. Votes of support.
† From *Shakespearean Tragedy: Lectures on Hamlet, Othello, King Lear, Macbeth* (London: Macmillan & Co., 1904), pp. 76–78.

or deride him as a busybody on the score of his rather theatrical satisfaction in the sensational conduct of his detective business: he is on
the whole a not unrighteous or ignoble justice, and not unworthy to
redeem the heroic object of his admiring affection from the threat-
ened stagnation of a cloister. But, superb as is all the tragic part of this
unique and singular play, it can be questioned only by the most ques-
tionable moralists that the comic part, lit up as it is by rare occasional
flashes of Shakespearean power (with a streak in it of Jonsonian bru-
tality), is generally far less humorous than usual, and decidedly not
less gross than the kindred scenes of brotherly in a play to which they
can have been contributed by no feebler hand than Shakespeare's.

G. WILSON KNIGHT

From The Wheel of Fire[†]

* * *

Measure for Measure *and the Gospels*

In *Measure for Measure* we have a careful dramatic pattern, a studied explication of a central theme: the moral nature of man in relation to the crudity of man's justice, especially in the matter of sexual
vice. There is, too, a clear relation existing between the play and the
Gospels, for the play's theme is this:

> Judge not, that ye be not judged. For with what judgement ye
> judge, ye shall be judged: and with what measure ye mete, it shall
> be measured to you again. (Matthew, vii. I)

The ethical standards of the Gospels are rooted in the thought of
Measure for Measure. Therefore, in this analysis we shall, while fix-
ing attention primarily on the play, yet inevitably find a reference to
the New Testament continually helpful, and sometimes essential.

Measure for Measure is a carefully constructed work. Not until we
view it as a deliberate artistic pattern of certain pivot ideas deter-
mining the play's action throughout shall we understand its peculiar
nature. Though there is consummate psychological insight here and
at least one person of most vivid and poignant human interest, we
must first have regard to the central theme, and only second look for
exact verisimilitude to ordinary processes of behaviour. We must be
careful not to let our human interest in any one person distort our

† From *The Wheel of Fire: Interpretations of Shakespearian Tragedy with Three New Essays*
(London: Methuen & Co. Ltd., 1949), pp. 73–74, 76–78, 89–96. Reprinted by permission of Taylor & Francis Books UK.

Lucio traduces the Duke's character, Mistress Overdone informs against Lucio. Barnadine is universally despised. All, that is, react to each other in an essentially ethical mode: which mode is the peculiar and particular vision of this play. Even music is brought to the bar of the ethical judgement:

> . . . music oft hath such a charm
> To make bad good, and good provoke to harm.   (IV. i. 16)

Such is the dominating atmosphere of this play. Out of it grow the main themes, the problem and the lesson of *Measure for Measure*. There is thus a pervading atmosphere of orthodoxy and ethical criticism, in which is centred the mysterious holiness, the profound death-philosophy, the enlightened human insight and Christian ethic of the protagonist, the Duke of Vienna.

The satire of the play is directed primarily against self-conscious, self-protected righteousness. The Duke starts the action by resigning his power to Angelo. He addresses Angelo, outspoken in praise of his virtues, thus:

> Angelo,
> There is a kind of character in thy life,
> That to the observer doth thy history
> Fully unfold. Thyself and thy belongings
> Are not thine own so proper, as to waste
> Thyself upon thy virtue, they on thee.
> Heaven doth with us as we with torches do;
> Not light them for themselves; for if our virtues
> Did not go forth of us, 'twere all alike
> As if we had them not. Spirits are not finely touch'd,
> But to fine issues, nor Nature never lends
> The smallest scruple of her excellence,
> But, like a thrifty goddess, she determines
> Herself the glory of a creditor,
> Both thanks and use.   (I. i. 27)

The thought is similar to that of the Sermon on the Mount:

> Ye are the light of the world. A city that is set on an hill cannot be hid. Neither do men light a candle, and put it under a bushel, but on a candle-stick; and it giveth light unto all that are in the house.   (Matthew, v. 14)

Not only does the Duke's 'torch' metaphor clearly recall this passage, but his development of it is vividly paralleled by other of Jesus' words. The Duke compares 'Nature' to a creditor', lending qualities and demanding both 'thanks and use'. Compare:

The last act of judgement is heralded by trumpet calls:

> Twice have the trumpets sounded;
> The generous and gravest citizens
> Have hent the gates, and very near upon
> The Duke is entering.   (IV. vi. 12)

So all are, as it were, summoned to the final judgement. Now Angelo, Isabella, Lucio—all are understood most clearly in the light of this scene. The last act is the key to the play's meaning, and all difficulties are here resolved. I shall observe the judgement measured to each, noting retrospectively the especial significance in the play of Lucio and Isabella.

Lucio is a typical loose-minded, vulgar wit. He is the product of a society that has gone too far in condemnation of human sexual desires. He keeps up a running comment on sexual matters. His very existence is a condemnation of the society which makes him a possibility. Not that there is anything of premeditated villainy in him: he is merely superficial, enjoying the unnatural ban on sex which civilization imposes, because that very ban adds point and spice to sexual gratification. He is, however, sincerely concerned about Claudio, and urges Isabella to plead for him. He can be serious—for a while. He can speak sound sense, too, in the full flow of his vulgar wit:

> Yes, in good sooth, the vice is of a great kindred; it is well allied: but it is impossible to extirp it quite, friar, till eating and drinking be put down. They say this Angelo was not made by man and woman after this downright way of creation: is it true, think you?
> (III. ii. 110)

This goes to the root of our problem here. Pompey has voiced the same thought (II. i. 248–63). This is, indeed, what the Duke has known too well: what Angelo and Isabella do not know. Thus Pompey and Lucio here at least tell downright facts—Angelo and Isabella pursue impossible and valueless ideals. Only the Duke holds the balance exact throughout. Lucio's running wit, however, pays no consistent regard to truth. To him the Duke's leniency was a sign of hidden immorality:

> Ere he would have hanged a man for getting a hundred bastards, he would have paid for the nursing of a thousand: he had some feeling of the sport; he knew the service, and that instructed him to mercy.   (III. ii. 126)

He traduces the Duke's character wholesale. He does not pause to consider the truth of his words. Again, there is no intent to harm—merely a careless, shallow, truthless wit-philosophy which enjoys its own sex-chatter. The type is common. Lucio is refined and vulgar, and the more vulgar because of his refinement; whereas Pompey, because

> a more strict restraint
> Upon the sisterhood, the votarists of Saint Clare. (I. iv. 4)

Even Lucio respects her. She calls forth something deeper than his usual wit:

> I would not—though 'tis my familiar sin
> With maids to seem the lapwing and to jest,
> Tongue far from heart—play with all virgins so:
> I hold you as a thing ensky'd and sainted,
> By your renouncement an immortal spirit,
> And to be talk'd with in sincerity,
> As with a saint.   (I. iv. 31)

Which contains a fine and exact statement of his shallow behaviour, his habitual wit for wit's sake. Lucio is throughout a loyal friend to Claudio: truer to his cause, in fact, than Isabella. A pointed contrast. He urges her to help. She shows a distressing lack of warmth. It is Lucio that talks of 'your poor brother'. She is cold:

> LUCIO.   Assay the power you have.
> ISABELLA.   My power? Alas, I doubt—
> LUCIO.   Our doubts are traitors
>   And make us lose the good we oft might win,
>   By fearing to attempt.   (I. iv. 76)

Isabella's self-centred saintliness is thrown here into strong contrast with Lucio's manly anxiety for his friend. So, contrasted with Isabella's ice-cold sanctity, there are the beautiful lines with which Lucio introduces the matter to her:

> Your brother and his lover have embraced:
> As those that feed grow full, as blossoming time
> That from the seedness the bare fallow brings
> To teeming foison, even so her plenteous womb
> Expresseth his full tilth and husbandry.   (I. iv. 40)

Compare the pregnant beauty of this with the chastity of Isabella's recent lisping line:

> Upon the sisterhood, the votarists of Saint Clare. (I. iv. 5)

Isabella lacks human feeling. She starts her suit to Angelo poorly enough—she is luke-warm:

> There is a vice that most I do abhor,
> And most desire should meet the blow of justice;
> For which I would not plead but that I must;
> For which I must not plead, but that I am
> At war 'twixt will and will not.   (II. ii. 29)

There is a suggestion that Angelo's strong passion has itself moved her, thawing her ice-cold pride. This is the moment of her trial: the Duke is watching her keenly, to see if she has learnt her lesson—nor does he give her any help, but deliberately puts obstacles in her way. But she stands the test: she bows to a love greater than her own saint-liness. Isabella, like Angelo, has progressed far during the play's action: from sanctity to humanity.

Angelo, at the beginning of this final scene, remains firm in denial of the accusations levelled against him. Not till the Duke's disguise as a friar is made known and he understands that deception is no longer possible, does he show outward repentance. We know, however, that his inward thoughts must have been terrible enough—his earlier ago-nized soliloquies put this beyond doubt. Now, his failings exposed, he seems to welcome punishment:

> Immediate sentence then and sequent death
> Is all the grace I beg.   (V. i. 374)

Escalus expresses sorrow and surprise at his actions. He answers:

> I am sorry that such sorrow I procure:
> And so deep sticks it in my penitent heart
> That I crave death more willingly than mercy;
> 'Tis my deserving and I do entreat it.   (V. i. 475)

To Angelo, exposure seems to come as a relief: the horror of self-deception is at an end. For the first time in his life he is both quite honest with himself and with the world. So he takes Mariana as his wife. This is just: he threw her over because he thought she was not good enough for him,

> Partly for that her promised proportions
> Came short of composition, but in chief
> For that her reputation was disvalued
> In levity.   (V. i. 213)

He aimed too high when he cast his eyes on the sainted Isabel: now, knowing himself, he will find his true level in the love of Mariana. He has become human. The union is symbolical. Just as his supposed love-contact with Isabel was a delusion, when Mariana, his true mate, was taking her place, so Angelo throughout has deluded himself. Now his acceptance of Mariana symbolizes his new self-knowledge. So, too, Lucio is to find his proper level in marrying Mistress Kate Keepdown, of whose child he is the father. Horrified as he is at the thought, he has to meet the responsibilities of his profligate behaviour. The punish-ment of both is this only: to know, and to be, themselves. This is both their punishment and at the same time their highest reward for their sufferings: self-knowledge being the supreme, perhaps the only, good.

> O my dear lord,
> I crave no other nor no better man.   (V. i. 426)

She knows that

> best men are moulded out of faults,
> And, for the most, become much more the better
> For being a little bad.   (V. i. 440)

The incident is profoundly true. Love asks no questions, sees no evil, transfiguring the just and unjust alike. This is one of the surest and finest ethical touches in this masterpiece of ethical drama. Its moral of love is, too, the ultimate splendour of Jesus' teaching.

Measure for Measure is indeed based firmly on that teaching. The lesson of the play is that of Matthew, v. 20:

> For I say unto you. That except your righteousness shall exceed the righteousness of the scribes and Pharisees, ye shall in no case enter into the Kingdom of Heaven.

The play must be read, not as a picture of normal human affairs, but as a parable, like the parables of Jesus. The plot is, in fact, an inversion of one of those parables—that of the Unmerciful Servant (Matthew, xviii); and the universal and level forgiveness at the end, where all alike meet pardon, is one with the forgiveness of the Parable of the Two Debtors (Luke, vii). Much has been said about the difficulties of *Measure for Measure*. But, in truth, no play of Shakespeare shows more thoughtful care, more deliberate purpose, more consummate skill in structural technique, and, finally, more penetrating ethical and psychological insight. None shows a more exquisitely inwoven pattern. And, if ever the thought at first sight seems strange, or the action unreasonable, it will be found to reflect the sublime strangeness and unreason of Jesus' teaching.

J. W. LEVER

The Date of *Measure for Measure*†

The first recorded performance of *Measure for Measure* was in the banqueting hall at Whitehall on St. Stephen's Night, December 26, 1604.[1] There are, however, indications that the play may have been

---

† "*The Date of Measure for Measure*," *Shakespeare Quarterly*, 10 (1959), 381–88. © Folger Shakespeare Library. Reprinted with permission of The Johns Hopkins University Press. All notes are by Lever.
1. Revels Accounts: see E. K. Chambers, *William Shakespeare* (1930) II, 331.

summer of 1603. After the death-roll from plague in London during one week had mounted to 857,[5] the King very properly forbade public access to Westminster and sent the gentry back to their country homes. For the same reason, all coronation festivities were cancelled, the holding of Bartholomew Fair was prohibited, and the Michaelmas Term session of the courts was transferred to Winchester. As for the "inhibition" mentioned by Steevens, it is sufficient to quote the words in their context. They are taken from T. M.'s *A True Narration of the Entertainment of his Royal Maiestie, from the Time of his Departure from Edinburgh, till his Receiving in London*[6] and describe the king's action on April 15, 1603, on his way to York:

> His traine still encreasing by the numbers of Noblemen and Gen-tlemen from the South parts, that came to offer him fealtie, . . . whose loue though he greatly tendered, yet did their multitudes so oppresse the countrey, and make prouision so deare, that he was faine to publish an inhibition. . . . [7]

This rout of noblemen and gentlemen hurrying north in hope of liq-uid refreshment at the fount of honor, where titles were being show-ered upon all comers, was of a very different social composition from "the general", or common people, to whom Steevens and Malone made the quotation apply.

There is indeed no evidence at all that the new king took offence at the crowd's display of enthusiasm during his journey through En-gland in the spring of 1603. Rather it seemed as if king and people were vying with one another in the display of affection. T. M.'s nar-rative presents a vivid picture of this halcyon time. When on April 6th, James crossed the border and entered Berwick,

> the common people seemed so ouer-wrapt with his presence, that they omitted nothing their power and capabilities could attaine vnto, to expresse loyall dutie and heartie affection: kneeling, shouting, crying, welcome, and God saue King *Iames,* till they were (in a maner) intreated to be silent.[8]

This plea for silence was to enable the recorder to read his prepared address. The festivities were organized by the mayor and civic digni-taries, and it is most unlikely that James, at his very first encounter with the people of England, would have objected to such a welcome. Certainly at Durham on April 11th he showed no distaste for public-ity. He went sight-seeing, and celebrated his coming by freeing all

5. The figure given in Stow's *Annales* (ed. 1615), p. 827, col. 2.
6. Reprinted in John Nichols, *The Progresses of King James I* (1828) I, 53–120, and C. H. Firth, *Stuart Tracts* 1603–1693 (*An English Garner*) (Westminster, 1903), pp. 11–52.
7. Sig. D2 (Nichols, I, 76).
8. Sig. C2 (Nichols, I, 64).

closely"[5] to Whitehall—evidently thinking better now of his gesture at York—and journeyed by water to the Tower. Thereafter he stayed at Greenwich and Windsor until the week of the coronation in late July, when the spread of the plague gave ample reason for putting an effective barrier between the court and the citizenry.

What James may have remarked in court circles about the exuberance of the people is unrecorded, and would have little chance of reaching the ears of the public during the mass exodus from London at this time. For the coronation on July 25th only twelve representative citizens were present as a token attendance,[6] and the king made no more public appearances until the following spring. There was certainly no occasion for such overt display of annoyance as could warrant an otherwise highly impertinent "apology" from the stage. But by March 15, 1604, the plague was over in the capital and the grand ceremonial ride through London streets, planned for the previous year, could at last take place. Contemporary descriptions of that ride abound in details,[7] but none mentions any untoward incident. The crowds, though enormous, were kept behind rails and well marshalled by the city companies. Arthur Wilson, writing in 1653 under the Commonwealth, was an uninhibited critic of James I who never erred on the side of flattery. But he admits that on this occasion the king conducted himself well enough:

> He endured this day's brunt with patience, being assured that he should never have another, and his triumphal riding to the Parliament that followed. But afterwards in his publick appearances (especially in his sports) the accesses of the people made him so impatient, that he often dispersed them with frowns, that we may not say with curses.[8]

James's dislike of the people's "untaught love" would seem to have become common knowledge only some time after March, if Wilson is to be believed. But it happens that the very occasion when offence was, for the first time, unequivocally expressed in public has been recorded. Gilbert Dugdale's *The Time Triumphant*, entered in Stationers' Register on March 27, 1604,[9] is an interesting little tract. As an eye-witness account of the royal progress of March 15th, it supplies a number of details unmentioned elsewhere. The author also goes out of

---

5. Stow, p. 824, col. I (T. M. has "going quietly on horsebacke," sig. G2, which has presumably been corrected in Stow's *Annales*).

6. Stow, *Abridgement* (1618), p. 445.

7. E.g., Dekker, *The Magnificent Entertainment* (1604) (Nichols, I, 337–76), Ben Jonson, *The Kings Entertainment* (1604) (Nichols, I, 377–99; ed. Herford and Simpson, VII, 83–109), Drayton, *A Paean Triumphall* (1604) (Nichols, I, 402–407).

8. Arthur Wilson, *The History of Great Britain, Being the Life and Reign of King James the First* (1653), p. 13.

9. Reprinted in Nichols, I, 408–19, Firth, pp. 69–82.

tion; just so do the "foolish throngs" behave when they "quit their own part" to interfere with the movements of their "well-wisht King". The crowd was within its right when it stood in line on Cornhill, admiring the superb triumphal arch erected by the Flemish residents and cheering the King as he passed—with Shakespeare and his fellow-actors in their new red livery not far behind. Its offence has been to stream from its proper place, like Angelo's blood at the sight of Isabella, and press upon the King, the heart of the nation. It becomes clear that the images of the passage in *Measure for Measure* are carefully inter-related, and that the last lines from "and euen so" to "offence", are not a hasty post-script, but a planned conclusion to Angelo's speech.

Dugdale's other publication, *A True Discourse of the practices of Elizabeth Caldwell*, the account of an attempted murder in Cheshire, was entered in Stationers' Register on June 11th, 1604, less than three months after *The Time Triumphant*. It contains two dedicatory epistles, one addressed to Lady Mary Cholmsley and a long list of Cheshire gentlemen by their "kind poore Countryman Gilbert Dugdale, engaged to you all in debt and dutie".[2] Dugdale claims to have resided for a long time in Chester and to have been there up to the date of Elizabeth Caldwell's execution on June 18, 1603, but to be in London at the time of writing. The other epistle has long been a recognized document in stage history.[3] It is addressed to Lady Chandos by Robert Armin, the famous clown who was at that time a sharer in Shakespeare's company, and supplies evidence that he had previously been associated with the Chandos household. Vouching for the truth of the account ostensibly given by Dugdale, Armin writes:

> so it was, and for the better proofe that it was so, I haue placed my kinsmans name to it, who was present . . . [4]

He concludes by offering "my true ensuing storie".[5] Evidently there was collaboration between the two kinsmen, Dugdale and Armin, with a strong likelihood that Armin "wrote up" the description of the attempt at murder from Dugdale's account. It may be asked whether *The Time Triumphant* was not put together in comparable fashion. Armin was an experienced journalist, whereas the only two publications connected with Dugdale are these two small tracts, appearing within three months of one another while Dugdale was staying in London. Armin, taking part in the royal progress as one of the King's

2. *A True Discourse*, sig. A3.
3. See *The Works of Robert Armin, Actor*, ed. Alexander Grosart (limited edition) (1880) I, pp. vi, ix, with Armin's epistle reprinted on pp. x–xi; Austin K. Gray, "Robert Armine the Foole", PMLA (1927) XLII, 678, 680; Edwin Nungezer, *A Dictionary of Actors* (New Haven 1929), p. 17. I am indebted to Mr. John Crow for the first two references.
4. *A True Discourse*, sig. D4 (Grosart, p. x).
5. Sig. D4ᵛ (Grosart, p. xi).

of the tribute, and in the recognition of the political and diplomatic equality of the two contracting Powers. Though more or less transitory in its effects, it was the first "peace with honour" concluded by a Habsburg Emperor with his arch-foe. (P. 701)

With this misconception removed, the First Gentleman's dislike of the "King of *Hungaries* peace" may be transferred to a more probable time and situation—the summer of 1604 and the negotiations with the King of Spain and the Archdukes of the Austrian Netherlands for an end to the war which had continued for two decades. In his speech to Parliament on March 19th, James stated his intention to discuss peace terms; on May 20th the Commissioners of the three states met in London; and on August 19th 1604, after some period of uncertainty, James ratified the peace treaty. It was proclaimed between King James and

> the High and mighty Prince Philip the 3. of that name, K. of Spaine, &c. and Albert and Isabell, Archdukes of Austria, dukes of Burgundy, &c.[8]

Archdukes or dukes were much in the news all summer: hence probably Lucio's hitherto unexplained reference to "the other dukes"; while the name of Isabella, joint ruler of Austria, may not be without relevance to Shakespeare's play. These negotiations were of much concern to the more ebullient gentlemen-about-town, whose prospects were bound up with a continuation of the war. As Stow commented:

> This peace was more ioyfully accepted then the people made shew for, by reason the multitude of pretended gallants, banckrouts, and vnruly youths weare at this time setled in pyracie accompting whatsoeuer they got, good purchase, ...

The description well suits Lucio and his companions, and explains the turn of thought which prompted the joke about the "sanctimonious pirat". However, the play's setting is still in a time of war, as Mistress Overdone's comments in the same scene make clear, and the First Gentleman's prayer that peace might not "break out" would have been overtaken by events after August 19th.

The censorship would not, of course, permit overt discussion on the stage of actual peace negotiations in progress. As Louis Albrecht suggested,[9] this had to be decently veiled by talk of a fictitious dispute between a king of Hungary and certain unnamed dukes. The references were suitably vague: soldiers of fortune had served for many years in Hungary in the wars of the Empire; history offered many examples of

---

8. Stow, *Annales*, p. 845, col. 2.
9. *Neue Untersuchungen zu Shakespeares Mass für Mass* (Berlin, 1914), pp. 216 ff.

King's Players, in which James seems to have been impersonated on the stage, was mentioned in a letter dated December 18, 1604.[5] But this hardly accords with de Beaumont's reference to a comedy that the queen attended *exprez pour s'en rire;* nor is it conceivable that such a treatment of the Gowry story would have been permitted, even allowing for the discrepancy of dates. It is more likely that the play mentioned on June 7, 1604, was Shakespeare's *Measure for Measure,* whose politic Duke in so many ways resembled James I. As a foreigner, de Beaumont might have misconstrued reports of the amusing passages between Lucio and the Duke, and taken these for seditious lampoons against the king. If so, we have here a contemporary record of the date of performance which is in perfect agreement with the evidence already considered.

ROSALIND MILES

From The Problem of *Measure for Measure*[†]

*   *   *

Any survey of the themes of *Measure for Measure* will demonstrate their seriousness and importance. It will not, however, support that interpretation of the play which finds its heart and meaning in the Duke. At the conclusion, as with the development of the themes as a whole, to take the Duke as the whole centre, and as the successful centre of *Measure for Measure,* will not answer to our experience of this drama. He is important, tremendously so; but not, as has often been asserted by enthusiasts, totally and engrossingly important.

There are several possible explanations for this. One is that the attractions of the *via media* have always been notoriously difficult to convey, and it may be argued in Shakespeare's defence that the golden mean is an intrinsically undramatic theme. It can easily be overshadowed by the extravagances and excesses, the profound statements and absurd gestures, of comedy and tragedy. To see the Duke placidly and prosaically achieving his unquestionably humane aims holds little interest in comparison with the spectacle of three unusually intense characters tearing each other to pieces. Morally, our sympathies should be with the Duke, but many readers and spectators are often far away on an imaginary Roman holiday, dreaming of the butchery they have missed.

5. Chambers, II, 330.
† From *The Problem of* Measure for Measure: *A Historical Investigation* (New York: Barnes & Noble, 1976). Reprinted by permission.

convention of drama that "good" characters bear the main thematic burden of a play, and that their statements represent the author's conclusions. This is a sound and practical device, since we are more likely to be receptive to characters whom we like and approve than to those who frighten or repel. It is possible that the frequency of this practice tends to obscure what is happening in an intricately-made play like *Measure for Measure*. We may feel that Shakespeare's "real thoughts" are only expressed through characters who are honourable, kind, and usually getting on in years, and it may be considered ill-advised to place too much thematic value on the remarks of comic and morally disreputable characters like Pompey. But, as we have seen at some length, the truths of *Measure for Measure* are not located only in the fine arias of Isabella or the pronouncements of the Duke. A character like Pompey can never be as eloquent or as lengthy in the statement of his attitudes, but his contribution is equally important, because through such characters the dramatist achieves a far more precise balance in the management of his themes. The comments of Pompey are as valuable as those of the Duke in creating the total impression.

Shakespeare does not attempt to persuade us by making us like or respect the characters who seem to share the thematic responsibility and who deliver the pronouncements which could be taken to contain the author's conclusions. There is no principal character in *Measure for Measure* whom we can like or identify with; the Duke, Angelo, and Isabella, all seem in their various ways too self-absorbed and narrow to arouse the affection of an audience. Consequently we are forced by Shakespeare to take each character on its own terms. We have also to cope with astonishing emotional somersaults from Angelo and Isabella, and some very brisk manoeuvring from the Duke, so that we have to learn to hold our responses in suspension from scene to scene. We can never allow our expectations to crystallise, or we are sure to be disappointed.

Measure for Measure may then be one of the rare plays which does not provide any clear point of reference for its audience. This lack of a fixed centre is one of the reasons why *Measure for Measure* is such a problematical drama, and why so many contrasting and contradictory interpretations are possible. With this drama every reader is on his own to make what he can of it, and the ironic spirit of the author has led him to remove most of the helpful or reassuring pointers which we can usually expect of a play. Shakespeare tries to chart the Duke's mistakes, his partial growth of self-knowledge and the knowledge of others, and his final adoption of the middle path between extremes. The development of the Duke forms the pattern for that of the other two principals Angelo and Isabella, and to a lesser extent of Claudio and even of Juliet. The unfolding of these characters reflects that of the Duke and coincides with it; indeed almost all the characters in the

For paradoxically one might say that Shakespeare's compassion springs directly from his ironic detachment. In *Measure for Measure* he has created a set of generally unlovable people, and he directs us throughout not to make judgements on them. In the end we should be able to make allowances for the most venal, self-indulgent, or wrong-headed of them, whether we like them or not. The play often seems to be in this respect a preliminary essay on one of the *Lear* themes, "Use every man after his desert, and who should 'scape whipping?" This question from *Hamlet*, with its wry, almost cynical note, its realism and its understanding, aptly catches what one may feel to be the characteristic tone of its successor, *Measure for Measure*.

This approach is persuasive; we might almost say complete. Yet, as I have said earlier, all this represents the play rather as it might have been than as it is. This account comes closer to describing our feelings about *Measure for Measure* than the argument which insists on the Duke as the powerful and successful centre of the whole structure. But even this does not answer to the facts. We cannot accept the Duke simply as part of the ironic whole, if only because it is impossible to be certain about the quality or even the extent of the irony which is directed at him. Rarely can we see that any of the Duke's acts or statements are clearly, if implicitly, rebuked. We have seen the guarded nature of Shakespeare's treatment of the Duke's early laxity, his withdrawal from ruling, his manner, and his treatment of the other characters. From time to time we may feel, as we do in the scene with Juliet, that the Duke is being deliberately presented as pompous and rather inadequate. At other times it is possible—one cannot be certain—that what may appear pomposity may in fact be consciously exploited by the Duke as an ironic mask; and at times, too, particularly in the final scene, it is clear that the Duke is enjoying an ironic awareness of his situation at the expense of the other characters. At all events the constant fluctuation of tone in Shakespeare's treatment of the Duke is disconcerting in its capacity to leave us not knowing where we really stand, or in what spirit to respond to him.

There is no satisfactory resolution of our mixed feelings towards the Duke. In the last act he is more impressive than he has been before, but we do not feel that the Duke of the end is a new and improved version of the one before; his former inadequacies may be gone, but they are not forgotten. All this is an expression of the fact that Shakespeare did not finally know what to do with his Duke. The ironic focus is flickering and uncertain throughout, and it dies at the end because Shakespeare needed the Duke as a simple figure of authority, to manipulate the conclusion, and to make the play's thematic point.

It would seem, then, that the simplistic handling of the Duke in the latter part of *Measure for Measure* marks an attempt by Shakespeare

Shakespeare's treatments are not always *simply better* than those of others. His problems with the stock pieces of Elizabethan and Jacobean drama seem to arise from his attempt to rework, in his own unique terms, a series of characters and devices which his own age had turned to other, sometimes more dramatically satisfying, uses. It is my contention that in Shakespeare's own day, his audience could have been as puzzled and unsatisfied by *Measure for Measure* as modern audiences often are; and that subsequent critical dislike or disapproval may often be vindicated, even at what have seemed its weakest points.

Nor should we need to shrink from this conclusion. We have all been made afraid, notably by F. R. Leavis, more recently perhaps by David Lloyd Stevenson, of admitting to any unease with *Measure for Measure*. But the efforts of the dons, however worthy or distinguished, cannot be allowed to crush the evidence of the stage, where it has never been popular, of the contemporary writers, or of our own common sense and humanity. We cannot make the play great simply by asserting that it is so. Nor can we shore up its rickety plot-structure by invoking a medievalism which in this case is false. Consider some of Shakespeare's unquestioned masterpieces, either in the comic or tragic form; *As You Like It,* say, or *Macbeth,* or even the "mixed" *Tempest.* How often, in these cases, do we have to correct our response with "Ah yes, but in 1604 . . ."? This in itself implies that the method has failed, for ideally historical association should be invoked to deepen understanding and increase delight. It should not inhibit personal response, nor should it be a prerequisite to comprehension.

The conventions of seventeenth-century drama are perfectly adequate to the creation of full, harmonious, and undeniably great plays like *Hamlet* or *The Winter's Tale.* We have then to admit the possibility that if a play fails, it fails in a wider context than ours. Rehabilitation based on reference to the conventions runs the constant risk of being both false and irrelevant, and there is a danger that this use of the historical method may become academic in the worst sense of the word. At best it can only take us so far; at worst, it can intimidate us into revering works which our natural inclinations might well lead us to rate far lower.

This should not be taken to imply a demand for the rejection of the historical method. Its real value lies in that it can, for instance, supply a frame of reference for Shakespeare's particular achievement by giving some idea of what contemporary dramatists could and did achieve. A study of these other dramas of the Elizabethan and Jacobean period remains valid as an aid to a more precise definition of what Shakespeare is offering in *Measure for Measure,* of what he is attempting to do, and how far he is successful. But this method gives only a comparative estimate and a comparative estimate is not absolute. Even

JONATHAN DOLLIMORE

Transgression and Surveillance
in *Measure for Measure*†

In the Vienna of *Measure for Measure* unrestrained sexuality is ostensibly subverting social order; anarchy threatens to engulf the State unless sexuality is subjected to renewed and severe regulation. Such at least is the claim of those in power. Surprisingly critics have generally taken them at their word even while dissociating themselves from the punitive zeal of Angelo. There are those who have found in the play only a near tragic conflict between anarchy and order, averted in the end it is true, but unconvincingly so. Others, of a liberal persuasion and with a definite preference for humane rather than authoritarian restraint, have found at least in the play's 'vision' if not precisely its ending an ethical sense near enough to their own. But both kinds of critic have apparently accepted that sexual transgression in *Measure for Measure*—and in the world—represents a real force of social disorder intrinsic to human nature and that the play at least is about how this force is—must be—restrained.

J. W. Lever, in an analysis of the play noted for its reasonableness,[1] draws a comparison with Shakespeare's romantic comedies where disorders in both society and individual, especially those caused by 'the excesses of sentiment and desire' are resolved: 'not only the problems of lovers, but psychic tensions and social usurpations or abuses, found their resolution through the exercise of reason, often in the form of an adjudication by the representatives of authority'. In *Measure for Measure* the same process occurs but more extremely: 'Not only are the tensions and discords wrought up to an extreme pitch, threatening the dissolution of all human values, but a corresponding and extraordinary emphasis is laid upon the role of true authority, whose intervention alone supplies the equipoise needed to counter the forces of negation'. Lever draws a further contrast with *Troilus and Cressida* where 'no supreme authority exists; age and wisdom can only warn, without stemming the inevitable tide of war and lechery'. On this view then unruly desire is extremely subversive and has to be countered by 'true' and 'supreme authority', 'age and wisdom', all of which qualities are possessed by the Duke in *Measure for Measure* and used by him to

---

† Published in *Political Shakespeare: New Essays in Cultural Materialism* (Ithaca, N.Y.: Cornell University Press, 1985), pp. 72–87. Copyright © Manchester University Press 1985. Used by permission of the publisher, Cornell University Press and the University of Manchester Press.

1. *Measure for Measure*, ed. J. W. Lever (London: Methuen, 1965).

Fie, sirrah, a bawd, a wicked bawd;
The evil that thou causest to be done,
That is thy means to live. Do thou but think
What 'tis to cram a maw or clothe a back
From such a filthy vice. Say to thyself,
From their abominable and beastly touches
I drink, I eat, array myself, and live.
Canst thou believe thy living is a life,
So stinkingly depending? (III.ii.18–26)

This is in response to Pompey's observation that such exploitation not only exists at other levels of society but is actually protected 'by order of law' (l. 8). This is just what the Duke's diatribe ignores— cannot acknowledge—fixating instead on the 'filthy vice' and its agents in a way which occludes the fact that it is Angelo, not Pompey, who, unchecked, and in virtue of his social position, will cause most 'evil . . . to be done'. But, because Angelo's transgression is represented as growing from his desire rather than his authority, his is a crime which can be construed as a lapse into the corruption of a lower humanity, a descent of the ruler into the sins of the ruled. Provocatively, his crime is obscurely theirs.

If we can indeed discern in the demonising of sexuality a relegitimation of authority we should not then conclude that this is due simply to an ideological conspiracy; or rather it may indeed be conspiratorial but it is also ideological in another, more complex sense: through a process of displacement an imaginary—and punitive— resolution of real social tension and conflict is attempted.

The authoritarian demonising of deviant behaviour was common in the period, and displacement and condensation—to and around low life—were crucial to this process (see also Paul Brown's analysis on these lines in the previous chapter). But what made displacement and condensation possible was a prior construction of deviancy itself. So, for example, diatribes against promiscuity, female self-assertion, cross-dressing and homosexuality construed these behaviours as symptomatic of an impending dissolution of social hierarchy and so, in effect, of civilisation.[3] This was partly because transgression was conceived in public and even cosmic terms; it would not then have made sense to see it in, say, psychological or subjective terms—a maladjustment of the individual who, with professional assistance, could be 'normalised'. On the one hand then homosexuality was not considered to be the 'defect' of a particular personality type since

---

3. Alan Bray, *Homosexuality in Renaissance England* (London: Gay Men's Press, 1982); Stuart Clark, 'Inversion, Misrule and the Meaning of Witchcraft', *Past and Present*, 87 (1980), 98–127; Christopher Hill, *The World Turned Upside Down: Radical Ideas During the English Revolution* (Harmondsworth: Penguin, 1975).

Their coexistence made for a complex social moment as well as a complex play.

J. A. Sharpe's recent and scrupulous study of crime in seventeenth-century England confirms this discrepancy between the official depiction of moral collapse among the lower orders and their actual behaviour. Sharpe also confirms that the suppression of sexuality was only 'one aspect of a wider desire to achieve a disciplined society. Fornication, like idleness, pilfering, swearing and drunkenness, was one of the distinguishing activites of the disorderly'. Further, the Elizabethan and early Stuart period marked an historical highpoint in an authoritarian preoccupation with the disorderly and their efficient prosecution.[7] Nevertheless, many of those concerned with this prosecution really did believe standards were declining and the social fabric disintegrating. Puritan extremists like Stubbes saw prostitution as so abhorrent they advocated the death penalty for offenders (Lever, p. xlvi). But if, as Stone and others argue, this fervour is the result of insecurity in the face of change, then, even if that fervour was 'sincere', the immorality which incited it was not at all its real cause. This is one sense in which the discourse of blame involved displacement; but there was another: while the authorities who actually suppressed the brothels often exploited the language of moral revulsion it was not the sexual vice that worried them so much as the meeting together of those who used the brothels. George Whetstone was only warning the authorities of what they already feared when he told them to beware of 'haunts . . . in Allies, gardens and other obscure corners out of the common walks of the Magistrate' whose guests are 'masterless men, needy shifters, thieves, cutpurses, unthrifty servants, both serving men and prentices'.[8] Suppression was an attempt to regulate not the vice, nor, apparently, even the spread of venereal disease, but the criminal underworld.[9] Similarly, in *Measure for Measure*, the more we attend to the supposed subversiveness of sexual licence, and the authoritarian

6. Lawrence Stone, *The Family Sex and Marriage in England 1500–1800* (London: Weidenfeld and Nicolson, 1977), pp. 653, 217, 654, 623–4; and F. G. Emmison has estimated that in the county of Essex around 15,000 people were summoned on sexual charges in the forty-five years up to 1603 (*Elizabethan Life: Morals and the Church Courts* (Chelmsford: Essex County Council, 1973), p. 1). Commenting on these figures Stone remarks that 'in an adult lifespan of 30 years, an Elizabethan inhabitant of Essex . . . had more than a one-in-four chance of being accused of fornication, adultery, buggery, incest, bestiality or bigamy' (*The Family*, p. 519).

7. J. A. Sharpe, *Crime in Seventeenth-Century England: a County Study* (Cambridge University Press, 1983), pp. 57, 70, 215–16.

8. *A Mirror for Magistrates* quoted from Thomas C. Izard's helpful study, *George Whetstone: Mid-Elizabethan Gentleman of Letters* (New York: Columbia University Press, 1942; reprinted New York: AMS Press, 1966), p. 140.

9. See the Proclamation of 1546 ordering London brothels to be closed, in *Tudor Royal Proclamations* (3 vols.), ed. Paul L. Hughes and James L. Larkin (New Haven: Yale University Press, 1964–9), I, 365–6; also Wallace Shugg, 'Prostitution in Shakespeare's London', *Shakespeare Studies* 10 (1977), 291–313, especially p. 306.

Yet those in power are sincerely convinced there is a threat to order. At the very outset of the play Escalus, described in the list of characters as an 'ancient' Lord, is praised excessively by the Duke only to be subordinated to Angelo, the new man. The traditional political 'art and practice' (I.i.12) of Escalus is not able to cope with the crisis. Later, the Duke, speaking to the Friar, acknowledges that this crisis stems from a failure on the part of the rulers yet at the same time displaces responsibility on to the ruled: like disobedient children they have taken advantage of their 'fond fathers' (I.iii.23). Hence the need for a counter-subversive attack on the 'liberty' of the low-life. Yet even as we witness that attack we see also that the possibilities for actual subversion seem to come from quite another quarter. Thus when Angelo resorts to the claim that the State is being subverted (in order to discredit charges of corruption against himself) the way he renders that claim plausible is most revealing:

> These poor informal women are no more
> But instruments of some more mightier member
> That sets them on. Let me have way, my lord,
> To find this practice out.   (V.i.235–7)

Earlier the Duke, pretending ignorance of Angelo's guilt, publicly denounces Isabella's charge against Angelo in similar terms:

>   thou knowest not what thou speak'st
> Or else thou art suborn'd against his honour
> In hateful practice . . .
>   . . . Someone hath set you on.   (V.i.108–10; 115)

The predisposition of Escalus to credit all this gives us an insight into how the scapegoat mentality works: just as the low-life have hitherto been demonised as the destructive element at the heart (or rather bottom) of the State, now it is the apparently alien Friar (he who is 'Not of this country', III.ii.211) who is to blame. The kind old Escalus charges the Friar (the Duke in disguise) with 'Slander to th'state!' and cannot wait to torture him into confession (V.i.320, 309–10). That he is in fact accusing the Duke ironically underpins the point at issue: disorder generated by misrule and unjust law (III.ii.6–8) is ideologically displaced on to the ruled—'ideologically' because Angelo's lying displacement is insignificant compared with the way that Escalus really believes it is the subordinate and the outsider who are to blame. Yet even as he believes this he is prepared to torture his way to 'the more mightier member' behind the plot; again there is the implication, and certainly the fear, that the origin of the problem is not intrinsic to the low-life but a hostile fraction of the ruling order.

Oddly the slander for which Escalus wants to have this outsider tortured, and behind which he perceives an insurrectionary plot, is only

high, much as a man might (then as now) blame a woman for tempt-
ing him sexually whereas in fact he has coerced her. The gentlemen
are 'mildly' reproached and restored to that which they have trans-
acted away while the low are disciplined. Whetstone believed that
the survival of England depended on its landed gentry; in rescuing
them from the low-life he is rescuing the State from chaos and restor-
ing it to its 'ancient and most laudable orders' (Izard, *George Whetstone*, p. 136). A reactionary programme is accomplished at the
expense of the low, while those who benefit are those responsible for
precipitating 'decline' in the first place. The same process of displacement occurs throughout discourses of power in this period.
One further example: one of the many royal proclamations attempting to bring vagabonds under martial law asserts that 'there can
grow no account of disturbance of our peace and quiet but from
such refuse and vagabond people' (*Tudor Royal Proclamations*, III,
233)—and this despite the fact that the proclamation immediately
preceeding this one (just six days before) announced the abortive
Essex rebellion. The failure of the rebellion is interpreted by the second proclamation as proof of the loyalty of all other subjects with
the exception of that 'great multitude of base and loose people' who
'lie privily in corners and bad houses, listening after news and stirs,
and spreading rumours and tales, being of likelihood ready to lay
hold of any occasion to enter into any tumult or disorder' (p. 232).
For the authoritarian perspective as articulated here, the unregulated are by definition the ungoverned and always thereby poten-
tially subversive of government. At the same time it is a perspective
which confirms what has been inferred from *Measure for Measure*:
in so far as the socially deprived were a threat to government this
was only when they were mobilised by powerful elements much
higher up the social scale. Moreover the low who were likely to be so
mobilised were only a small part of the 'base and loose people'
hounded by authority. In fact we need to distinguish, as Christopher
Hill does, between this mob element, little influenced by religious or
political ideology but up for hire, and the 'rogues, vagabonds and
beggars' who, although they 'caused considerable panic in ruling
circles . . . were incapable of concerted revolt' (*The World Turned
Upside Down*, pp. 40–1). Of course there were real social problems
and 'naturally' the deprived were at the centre of them. Moreover, if
we recall that there *were* riots, that fornication *did* produce charity
dependent bastards, that drunkenness *did* lead to fecklessness, it
becomes apparent that, in their own terms there were also real
grounds for anxiety on the part of those who administered depriva-
tion. At the same time we can read in that anxiety—in its very sur-
plus, its imaginative intensity, its punitive ingenuity—an ideological

unrepentant and even disinclined to escape; he thus offers no response on which the Duke might work to return him to a position of dutiful submission. But the Duke does not give up and resolves to 'Persuade this rude wretch willingly to die' (IV.iii.80; cf. II.i.35). A similar idea seems to be behind his determination to send Pompey to prison—not just to rot but for 'Correction and instruction' (III.ii.31). Earlier the Duke had been rather more successful with Claudio. His long 'Be absolute for death' speech (III.i.5ff) does initially return Claudio to a state of spiritual renunciation, but Claudio has not long been in conversation with Isabella before he desires to live again. Isabella, herself positioned in a state of intended renunciation, struggles to restore Claudio to his. She fails but the Duke intervenes again and Claudio capitulates.

The Duke makes of Mariana a model of dutiful subjection. Predictably, he is most successful with those who are least powerful and so most socially dependent. He tells Angelo to love Mariana, adding: 'I have confess'd her, and I know her virtue' (V.i.524). He has indeed, and earlier Mariana confirms his success in this confessional positioning of her as an acquiescent, even abject subject (IV.I.8–20); for her he is one 'whose advice / Hath often still'd my brawling discontent' (IV.i.8–9). His exploitation of her—'The maid will I frame, and make fit for his attempt' (III.i.256–7)—is of course just what she as confessed subject must not know, and the Duke confirms that she does not by eliciting from her a testimony:

DUKE: Do you persuade yourself that I respect you?
MARIANA: Good friar, I know you do, and so have found it
(IV.i.53–4)

Thus is her exploitation recast and indeed experienced by Mariana, as voluntary allegiance to disinterested virtue.

The Duke's strategy with Isabella is somewhat different. Some critics of the play, liking their women chaste, have praised Isabella for her integrity; others have reproached her for being too absolute for virtue.[6] Another assessment, ostensibly more sympathetic than either of these because psychological rather than overtly moralistic, is summarised by Lever. He finds Isabella ignorant, hysterical and suffering from 'psychic confusion', and he apparently approves the fact that 'through four . . . acts' she undergoes 'a process of moral education designed to reshape her character' (pp. lxxx, lxxvii, lxxix, xci). Here,

6. In the nineteenth century for example A. W. Schlegel praised 'the heavenly purity of her mind . . . not even stained with one unholy thought' and Edward Dowden her 'pure zeal' and 'virgin sanctity'. By contrast Coleridge found her 'unamiable' and Hazlitt reproved her 'rigid chastity'. These other passages from earlier critics are conveniently collected in C. K. Stead, ed., *Shakespeare: Measure for Measure, a Casebook* (London: Macmillan, 1971); see especially pp. 43–5, 59–62, 45–7, 47–9.

has departed he laments his inability to ensure his subject's dutiful respect: 'What king so strong / Can tie the gall up in the slanderous tongue?' (ll. 181–2; cf. IV.i.60–5). If the severity of the law at this time is anything to go by, such slander was a cause of obsessive concern to Elizabethan and Jacobean rulers,[7] just as it is here with the Duke and, as we have already seen, with Escalus.

The ideological representation of integrity can perhaps be judged best at the play's close—itself ideological but not, it seems to me, forced or flawed in the way critics have often claimed. By means of the Duke's personal intervention and integrity, authoritarian reaction is put into abeyance but not discredited: the corrupt deputy is unmasked but no law is repealed and the mercy exercised remains the prerogative of the same ruler who initiated reaction. The Duke also embodies a public reconciliation of law and morality. An omniscience, inseparable from seeming integrity, permits him to close the gulf between the two, one which was opening wide enough to demystify the one (law) and enfeeble the other (morality). Again, this is not a cancelling of authoritarianism so much as a fantasy resolution of the very fears from which authoritarianism partly grows—a fear of escalating disorder among the ruled which in turn intensifies a fear of impotence in the rulers. If so it is a reactionary fantasy, neither radical nor liberating (as fantasy may indeed be) but rather conservative and constraining; the very disclosure of social realities which make progress seem imperative is recuperated in comedic closure, a redemptive wish-fulfilment of the status quo.

In conclusion then the transgressors in *Measure for Measure* signify neither the unregeneracy of the flesh, nor the ludic subversive carnivalesque. Rather, as the spectre of unregulated desire, they are exploited to legitimate an exercise in authoritarian repression. And of course it is a spectre: desire, culturally manifested, is never unregulated, perhaps least of all in Jacobean London. Apart from their own brutally exploitative sub-cultural codes, the stews were controlled from above. This took several forms, including one of the most subtly coercive of all: economic investment. Some time between 1599 and 1602 the Queen's Lord Chamberlain, Lord Hunsdon, appears to have leased property for the establishing of an especially notorious brothel in Paris Gardens, while Thomas Nashe declared in 1598 that 'whoredom (the next doore to the Magistrates)' was set up and maintained through bribery, and Gāmini Salgādo informs us that 'Most theatre owners . . . were brothel owners too'.[8]

7. See especially Joel Samaha, 'Gleanings from Local Criminal Court Records: Sedition among the inarticulate in Elizabethan Essex', *Journal of Social History*, 8 (1975), 61–79.
8. E. J. Burford, *Queen of the Bawds* (London: Neville Spearman, 1974); Thomas Nashe, *The Unfortunate Traveller and Other Works*, ed. J. B. Steane (Harmondsworth: Penguin, 1972), p. 483; Gāmini Salgādo, *The Elizabethan Underworld* (London: Dent, 1977), p. 58.

notwithstanding, was one of the lucky ones; after all, the life of most prostitutes outside the exclusive brothels was abject. Overdone is at least a procuress, a brothel keeper. For most of the rest poverty drove them to the brothels and after a relatively short stay in which they had to run the hazards of disease, violence and contempt, most were driven back to it.

In pursuing the authority–subversion question, this chapter has tried to exemplify two complementary modes of materialist criticism. Both are concerned to recover the text's history. The one looks directly for history in the text including the historical conditions of its production which, even if not addressed directly by the text can nevertheless still be said to be within it, informing it. Yet there is a limit to which the text can be said to incorporate those aspects of its historical moment of which it never speaks. At that limit, rather than constructing this history as the text's unconscious, we might instead address it directly. Then at any rate we have to recognise the obvious: the prostitutes, the most exploited group in the society which the play represents, are absent from it. Virtually everything that happens presupposes them yet they have no voice, no presence. And those who speak for them do so as exploitatively as those who want to eliminate them. Looking for evidence of resistance we find rather further evidence of exploitation. There comes a time of course when the demonising of deviant sexuality meets with cultural and political resistance. From the very terms of its oppression deviancy generates a challenging counter-discourse and eventually a far-reaching critique of exploitation. That is another and later story.

KATHLEEN McLUSKIE

From The Patriarchal Bard: Feminist Criticism and Shakespeare: *King Lear* and *Measure for Measure*†

I

Every feminist critic has encountered the archly disingenuous question 'What exactly is feminist criticism?' The only effective response is 'I'll send you a booklist', for feminist criticism can only be defined by the multiplicity of critical practices engaged in by feminists. Owing its origins to a popular political movement, it reproduces the

† From *Political Shakespeare: New Essays in Cultural Materialism* (Ithaca, N.Y.: Cornell University Press, 1985), pp. 88–98, 106–07. Copyright © Manchester University Press 1985. Used by permission of the publisher, Cornell University Press and the University of Manchester Press.

Modern feminist psychoanalysis could be applied to Shakespearean characters for the texts were seen as unproblematically mimetic: 'Shakespeare and Freud deal with the same subject: the expressed and hidden feelings in the human heart. They are both psychologists.'[9] Shakespeare was thus constructed as an authoritative figure whose views about men and women could be co-opted to the liberal feminism of the critic. Within this critical practice, academic debate centred on conflicts over the authors' views rather than on the systems of representation or the literary traditions which informed the texts. Linda Bamber, for example, reminded her readers of the evident misogyny of Shakespeare's treatment of his tragic heroines and placed her own work 'in reaction against the tendency for feminist critics to interpret Shakespeare as if his work directly supports and develops feminist ideas'.[1] While noting the fundamental inconsistencies between Shakespeare's treatment of women in comedy and tragedy, she explicitly resists the temptation 'to revel in them offered by post-structuralism'. She finds instead a cohering principle in Shakespeare's recognition of women as 'other', which 'amounts to sexism only if the writer fails to attribute to opposite sex characters the privileges of the other'.[2] In tragedy his women are strong because they are coherent—'certainly none of the women in the tragedies worries or changes her mind about who she is'—and the attacks which are made on them are the product of male resentment at this strength—'misogyny and sex nausea are born of failure and self doubt'.[3] The comic feminine, on the other hand, is opposed not to men but to a reified 'society': 'In comedy the feminine either rebels against the restraining social order or (more commonly) presides in alliance with the forces which challenge its hegemony: romantic love, physical nature, the love of pleasure in all its forms.'[4]

These assertions rest on a reductive application of feminist anthropological discussions of nature and culture but their primary effect is to construct an author whose views can be applied in moral terms to rally and exhort the women readers of today: 'the comic heroines show us how to regard ourselves as other . . . the heroines laugh to see themselves absorbed into the ordinary human comedy; the heroes rage and weep at the difficulty of actually being as extraordinary as they feel themselves to be'.[5] These moral characteristics ascribed to men and women take no account of their particular circumstances within the texts, nor indeed of their material circumstances and the differential

9. *Ibid.*, p. 1.
1. Linda Bamber, *Comic Women, Tragic Men: a Study of Gender and Genre in Shakespeare* (Stanford: Stanford Univ. Press), p. 1.
2. *Ibid.*, p. 5.
3. *Ibid.*, p. 15.
4. *Ibid.*, p. 32.
5. *Ibid.*, p. 39.

the Hallers' essay on 'The puritan art of love',[9] she notes the shift from misogyny associated with Catholic asceticism to puritan assertions of the importance of women in the godly household as partners in holy and companionate marriage. The main portion of the book is an elaboration of themes—Chastity, Equality, Gods and Devils—in both polemic and dramatic literature. The strength of her argument lies in its description of the literary shift from the discourses of love poetry and satire to those of drama. However her assertions about the feminism of Shakespeare and his contemporaries depend once again upon a mimetic model of the relationship between ideas and drama. Contemporary controversy about women is seen as a static body of ideas which can be used or rejected by dramatists whose primary concern is not with parallel fictions but simply to 'explore the real nature of women'. By focusing on the presentation of women in puritan advice literature, Dusinberre privileges one side of a contemporary debate, relegating expressions of misogyny to the fictional world of 'literary simplification' and arbitrarily asserting more progressive notions as the dramatists' true point of view.[1]

A more complex discussion of the case would acknowledge that the issues of sex, sexuality, sexual relations and sexual division were areas of conflict of which the contradictions of writing about women were only one manifestation alongside the complexity of legislation and other forms of social control of sex and the family. The debates in modern historiography on these questions indicate the difficulty of assigning monolithic economic or ideological models to the early modern family, while the work of regional historians has shown the importance of specific material conditions on both the ideology and practice of sexual relations.[2] Far from being an unproblematic concept, 'the nature of women' was under severe pressure from both ideological discourses and the real concomitants of inflation and demographic change.

The problem with the mimetic, essentialist model of feminist criticism is that it would require a more multi-faceted mirror than Shakespearean drama to reflect the full complexity of the nature of women in Shakespeare's time or our own. Moreover this model

---

9. William Haller and Malleville Haller, 'The Puritan Art of Love', *Huntington Library Quarterly*, 5, (1942) 235–72. Cf. K. Davies, "The sacred condition of equality": how original were Puritan doctrines of marriage?' *Social History*, 5 (1977), 566–7.

1. Juliet Dusinberre, *op. cit.*, p. 183.

2. Chapter 4, 'Husbands and Wives, Parents and Children' of Keith Wrightson, *English Society 1580–1680* (London: Hutchinson, 1982) provides a comprehensively informed discussion of the controversy. See also Lawrence Stone, *The Family, Sex and Marriage in England, 1500–1800* (London: Weidenfeld and Nicolson, 1977); G. R. Quaife, *Wanton Wenches and Wayward Wives: Peasants and Illicit Sex in Early Seventeenth Century England* (London: Croom Helm, 1969); Margaret Spufford, *Contrasting Communities: English Villagers in the Sixteenth and Seventeenth Centuries* (Cambridge University Press, 1974).

limit the range of meaning which the text allows and circumscribe the position which a feminist reader may adopt *vis-à-vis* the treatment of gender relations and sexual politics within the plays. The feminist reader may resist the position which the text offers but resistance involves more than simple attitudinising.

II

In traditional criticism Shakespeare's plays are seldom regarded as the sum of their dramatic devices. The social location of the action, their visual dimension and the frequent claims they make for their own authenticity, invite an audience's engagement at a level beyond the plot. The audience is invited to make some connection between the events of the action and the form and pressure of their own world. In the case of sex and gender, the concern of feminists, a potential connection is presented between sexual relations as an aspect of narrative—who will marry whom and how?—and sexual relations as an aspect of social relations—how is power distributed between men and women and how are their sexual relations conducted? The process of interpretative criticism is to construct a social meaning for the play out of its narrative and dramatic realisation. However this is no straightforward procedure: the positions offered by the texts are often contradictory and meaning can be produced by adopting one of the positions offered, using theatrical production or critical procedures to close off others. The critic can use historical knowledge to speculate about the possible creation of meaning in the light of past institutions and ideologies but the gap between textual meaning and social meaning can never be completely filled for meaning is constructed every time the text is reproduced in the changing ideological dynamic between text and audience.

An interesting case in point is *Measure for Measure*, in which the conflicting positions offered by the text have resulted in critical confusion among those who wish to fix its moral meaning as the authentic statement of a coherent author. The problems have centred in large part on the narrative resolution in which the restoration of order through marriages seems both an affront to liberal sensibilities and an unsatisfactory suppression of the powerful passions evoked throughout the action. There seems to be an irresolvable gap between the narrative strategies—the bed-trick, the prince in disguise plot—and the realism of the other scenes in which we see 'corruption boil and bubble till it o'errun the stew'.

The relevance of discussions of early modern sexuality and social control is evident in the play's treatment of public regulation of morality. Nevertheless such historically informed attention as the play has main narrative line. The solution is imposed in this play by a figure from within the action, the all-powerful Duke, but it is no more inappropriate to the characters concerned than the finale of many another romantic comedy.

It is impossible to say how this resolution was regarded by Shakespeare's contemporaries. There is evidence to suggest that marriage was regarded as just such an instrument of effective social control and social harmony. However there is no reason why the elusive responses of past audiences need carry privileged status as the ultimate meaning of the text. The ideological struggle over sexuality and sexual relations which informs the text has emerged in different terms in the late twentieth century, and a liberal humanist reading of the text might present its social meaning as a despairing (or enthusiastic) recognition of the ineffectiveness of attempts at the control of such private, individual matters. A radical feminist production of the text could on the other hand, through acting, costume and style, deny the lively energy of the pimps and the bawds, foregrounding their exploitation of female sexuality. It might celebrate Isabella's chastity as a feminist resistance, making her plea for Angelo's life a gesture of solidarity to a heterosexual sister and a recognition of the difficulty of breaking the bonds of family relations and conventional sexual arrangements.

These different 'interpretations' are not, however, competing equals in the struggle for meaning. They each involve reordering the terms in which the text is produced, which of its conflicting positions are foregrounded, and how the audience response is controlled. In Jonathan Miller's production of the play, for example, Isabella literally refused the Duke's offer of marriage and walked off stage in the opposite direction. Miller has been a powerful advocate for the right of a director to reconstruct Shakespeare's plays in the light of modern preoccupations, creating for them an afterlife which is not determined by their original productions.[8] As a theatre director, he is aware of the extent to which the social meaning of a play depends upon the arrangements of theatrical meaning; which is different from simply asserting alternative 'interpretations'. The concept of interpretation suggests that the text presents a transparent view on to the real life of sexual relations whether of the sixteenth or the twentieth century. The notion of 'constructed meaning' on the other hand, foregrounds the theatrical devices by which an audience's perception of the action of the play is defined. The focus of critical attention, in other words, shifts from judging the action to analysing the process by which the action presents itself to be judged.

8. This idea was fully developed in Jonathan Miller's Eliot Lectures, 'The After Life of Plays' delivered at the University of Kent in 1978 (London: Faber and Faber, forthcoming).

Isabella, for all her importance in the play, is similarly defined theatrically by the men around her for the men in the audience. In the
scene of her first plea to Angelo, for example, she is physically framed
by Angelo, the object of her demand, and Lucio the initiator of her
plea. When she gives up after Angelo's first refusal, Lucio urges her
back with instructions on appropriate behaviour:

> Give't not o'er so. To him again! entreat him,
> Kneel down before him, hang upon his gown!
> You are too cold. (II.ii.43–5)

As her rhetoric becomes more impassioned, her speeches longer, our
view of her action is still dramatically mediated through Lucio
whose approving remarks and comic asides act as a filter both for
her action and for the audience's view of it.

Through Lucio and the provost the text makes us want her to win.
However, the terms of her victory are also defined by the rhetoric
and structure of the scene. A woman pleading with a man introduces
an element of sexual conflict which is made explicit in the bawdy
innuendo of Lucio's remarks (II.ii.123–4). The passion of the conflict, the sexualising of the rhetoric, and the engagement of the onstage
spectators create a theatrical excitement which is necessary to sustain
the narrative: it also produces the kind of audience involvement
which makes Angelo's response make sense. Like Angelo we are wit-
nesses to Isabella's performance so that we understand, if we do not
morally approve of, his reaction to it. It is, moreover, rendered theatrically valid in the heartsearching soliloquy which closes the
scene. His rhetorical questions 'Is this her fault or mine . . . Can it
be that modesty may more betray the sense / Than woman's lightness?' define the sexually appealing paradox of the passionate nun,
and the audience is intellectually engaged in his quandary by his
dilemma being put in the questioning form.

A feminist reading of the scene may wish to refuse the power of
Angelo's plea, may recognise in it the double bind which blames
women for their own sexual oppression. However to take up that
position involves refusing the pleasure of the drama and the text,
which imply a coherent maleness in their point of view.[2]

Isabella's dilemma is, by contrast, a pale affair. Her one soliloquy
deals only in the abstract opposition of chastity against her brother's
life. Her resounding conclusion 'Then Isobel live chaste and brother
die: / More than our brother is our chastity' (II.iv.184–5) offers no
parallel intellectual pleasures; it does not arise out of the passion of

---

2. Cf. the discussion of 'Reading as a Woman' in Jonathan Culler, *Theory and Criticism after
   Structuralism* (Ithaca: Cornell University Press, 1982), pp. 43–63. The implication there
   is that positioning the reader as a woman is a matter of free choice and the position
   adopted is coherent and determines clear cut readings.

ing year. In the same season (his first with the RSC) he also played Sir Andrew Aguecheek in *Twelfth Night* and Joe in Saroyan's *The Time of Your Life* at The Other Place. He has appeared on both sides of the Atlantic in a wide variety of stage, film, and television work, including *Macbeth* for the National Theatre and *Othello* (in which he played the title role) for Nottingham Playhouse. Other roles for the National Theatre were in Pinter's *Betrayal*, Shaw's *The Philanderer* and *Man and Superman*, Calderón's *The Mayor of Zalamea*, and Molière's *Le Malade Imaginaire*. His many television and film appearances include *War and Peace*, *The Golden Bowl*, *Roads to Freedom*, *Moll Flanders*, and *Star*.

It was one of the most difficult parts I've ever played, but it proved to be one of the most exciting experiences I've ever had in the theatre and it has hooked me to Shakespeare for life. Almost everyone else pales by comparison.

In the first place, Shakespeare is the ultimate examination for an actor. He is imaginatively bolder, takes greater risks in terms of character and narrative, explores the emotional and psychological parameters of a situation more comprehensively than anyone else, and all this in a language of either poetry or prose as compressed, exciting, and complex in thought and feeling as anywhere else in the English language: 'high astounding terms', in Marlowe's lovely phrase. But the problems are further compounded, in this instance, by the profoundly enigmatic nature of both this play, *Measure for Measure*, and the part of the Duke.

It is curious. In many ways the tone of the piece is very 'modern'— ironic and ambivalent, characters and narrative rife with contradiction, the themes a complex mixture of political and moral ambiguity. And yet the function of the institutions at the heart of the play, like the church and the state, have changed so ineradicably since Shakespeare's time that they can seem almost inaccessible to us now. God, in Shakespeare's time, was a living presence; you could be fined then for not going to church; suicide was the ultimate crime for the chilling reason that the culprit could no longer repent. In such an atmosphere a dilemma such as Isabella faces about whether to sleep with Angelo, condemn herself to eternal damnation but save her brother's life, is seething with painful irony and hair-raising moral danger. Today, some people find it in themselves to laugh at such goings on.

Again, in our democratic way of life, it must seem that the undreamed of autocratic power invested in the Duke is well nigh incomprehensible. He was King, judge, juror, and indeed the next best thing to God. And his power among his subjects would have seemed as natural and God-given as breath being drawn into a lung. So that the power of the play to speak to us now rested absolutely on more"' ('*Measure for Measure* and the Gospels', in *The Wheel of Fire*, 4th edn (London, 1949), p. 82).

Now it seems to me that the Duke's emotions get very much the better of him here—conflicting and contradictory emotions too. Anger, that his city has come to this; remorse, too, that he is in part responsible for it. In any case, the anger is almost explosive. And I believe the text of the speech supports me here. The active, transitive verbs at the end of the lines seem to propel him through the language with a kind of moral fury. By the end of the speech, incidentally, I used to seize hold of the chains wrapped around Pompey's body and shake him. I did it so violently one night that I caught the hairs on Tony O'Donnell's chest. And I have to confess that the sight of Pompey/O'Donnell's eyes crossing with the pain made a few repeat performances irresistible. I returned to my dressing room one night at the interval to find a Pompey bull nailed to the door on which was inscribed the message: 'O.K. Dukey! This is war!'

But I am, in any event, wary of the gentle Christ that seems to emerge in this kind of reading. There was a whole existential dimension to the man, born, as he was, to live a life on earth, with human appetites and human failings. I seem to remember that he overturned the tables of the money-changers in a state of abject fury. Whilst on the subject, I reject, too, the other side of the coin, that the Duke is an amoral manipulator of people's lives. I don't frankly think the text supports such a reading. There is a deal of plotting and scheming, it is true, but, behind the scheming, there is, always, the drive of high moral purpose. And to those who would argue that he is unnaturally obsessed with the necessity to make his scheme succeed, I would answer that he is playing for the highest stakes, playing indeed for his life and the moral regeneration of his city and his subjects. And in obsessions, ends justify means. He is, after all, dare I say it, merely human.

So, with decisions made about the basic political and social structure, the feel of how the play should be, what of the instincts and intuitions? I try to look for the reality and humanity. I suppose we all do. I found myself, in the previous paragraph, defending the Duke's obsession with the success of his scheme. Not as a justification, but because that was the way his nature responded to the situation. Who is to say, of course, that that is not the way *my* nature would have responded. Either way, I am encouraged by that impulse to defend what for some people would be a grave defect. Passing moral judgement, that is the curse, criticizing or manipulating from the outside, so to speak. For that could diminish, or even destroy, the contradictions of the character. I look for areas of the character that I can warm to, even love about him. In that way, you tend to avoid those out-of-date labels like good and bad. The person becomes more huge asset here too. Indeed, as I stepped out of the formal black breeches, frock-coat, buckle shoes and powdered wig into the simple monk habit, I really did feel an instant sense of physical and emotional freedom. I say simple habit: simple but heavy and hot. I felt, at first, as if I'd slipped into an Allied carpet. I remonstrated with Bob, who turned those lustrous Irish eyes on me with the words: 'Have you seen it in the mirror? You look wonderful.' I stayed in the carpet.

It should be remembered here, I think, that the Duke is at all times impersonating a friar. He has spent perhaps an hour or so with Friar Peter learning the monkish ropes, but, in reality, he would not be above forgetting himself once he sees the disguise working. Indeed, early on in rehearsals, in the long Act 2, Scene 1, I found that I tended to get perhaps a little too close to Juliet Stevenson's Isabella, to be touching her even. I was actually unaware of it. But Juliet noticed it and remarked upon it: 'You're supposed to be a friar.' She was right, of course, but in a way it was a natural instinct. The other important thing to remember about the Duke/friar disguise is that because of the exigencies of the scheme he is hatching he becomes a very fastidious moralist. Where he is the friar, he abruptly ceases to have any knowledge of the Duke, and vice versa. He is wonderfully adept at shedding one or the other's skin, let alone his mind. It becomes the key, really, to the successful conclusion of his designs.

Once out into the streets, he is in fact responding to events, unpleasant though they may be, that, in one way or another, he would have been expecting. It would be true to say that here he is on a kind of pastoral mission, helping the walking wounded. It is not really until he overhears the news about Angelo's duplicity that the plot of the play begins to overtake him (3.1.96ff). At this point he becomes a reactor to Angelo's mounting treachery. The schemes, if we must call them that, are his unequivocal response to that treachery, a desire to save the victims from the results of that treachery. In any event, the mood and pace of the whole play is irrevocably changed from that moment. It is almost as if a bomb has exploded in the street. From now on the play itself is, so to speak, 'under the whip' and there is also a clock of suspense permanently ticking away on the wall.

But before we go any further we must examine the wonderfully ambiguous area of the relationship between the Duke and Isabella which is just about to hatch. It must be said that there is not one vestige of a syllable, line, or comma, even, until 5.1.491 to suggest that there is anything between them at all. Nonetheless, Shakespeare being Shakespeare, it is frankly in the air, in the journey of the play, too. And of course, at the end of the play there is this unequivocal proposal. It is easier, at the end, for the Duke, because of that, than it is for Isabella. After a lot of difficulty (we were uncertain right through the previews) Juliet carried off what became a little miracle

At the end of this speech, if we had done our work properly, there was an audible whoop of satisfaction from the audience. The mounties were coming to the rescue! And all this in a man who, only hours before, was clamped inside his palace, imprisoned by his own power, seemingly incapable of embracing life or love, and powerless to help his subjects.

Fresh from this, we come now to the scene with Lucio. It is irresistible to a craftsman like Shakespeare. It accomplishes so much. Much needed comedy, for one thing. It advances the Duke's perceptions about himself, about his subjects and how they think of him, and for the fascinating Lucio it is the occasion for fizzling wit and fireworks. As to the vexed question of whether Lucio knows it is the Duke, I only know that if he plays the scene as if he does know, then the scene is as flat as a pancake. The scene, to my mind, is as perfect an example as you could find for demonstrating the magical properties of ambiguity. Does he or doesn't he know? Then the wit sparkles and the scene crackles with tension. If he does know, I am bound to ask what madness would then possess him, in the closing pages of the play, to tear the Duke's cowl from his head and unmask him? Lucio has many defects, but a passion for suicide is not one of them.

And then, as Lucio leaves, Escalus arrives upon the scene. Again, one marvels at the craftsmanship, at Shakespeare's ability to compress so much into the material by this subtle juxtaposition—the subject Lucio, revealing and infuriating by turns, and then his old friend, Escalus, a trusted adviser, the man whose gentleness and wisdom he had passed over, in favour of the flint-hard, cool-headed administrative genius. These are low moments, full of poignancy and even hopelessness. But contrast the following, with the thin and pedantic voice we heard at the beginning of the play; again, note the use of prose:

> ESCALUS What news abroad i' th' world?
>
> DUKE None, but that there is so great a fever on goodness, that the dissolution of it must cure it. Novelty is only in request, and it is as dangerous to be ag'd in any kind of course, as it is virtuous to be constant in any undertaking. There is scarce truth enough alive to make societies secure, but security enough to make fellowships accurs'd. Much upon this riddle runs the wisdom of the world.
>
> (3.2.221–9)

As bleak and chilling a vision as you would dare to find, but within it, it seems to me, there is the thought, already, of resolution. A moment later, only, Escalus quizzes him about Claudio, whom Escalus would dearly love to see saved. The Duke silences him, the integrity of his secret moral purpose superbly intact. I find this to be one of

fully useful laugh because it brought us the audience's total involvement in the story.

While the two girls go upstage to talk, the Duke is left downstage,
and it is here, in the text, that he is given a speech of some half-
dozen lines (4.1.59ff) that seem to have no connection with what is
going on in the scene at all. I am myself convinced that, at some point,
and for some unfathomable reason, they were filched from the soliloquy of the Duke following the exit of Lucio at 3.2.184, where they
make total sense, and it is to that moment in the play that we restored
them. I knelt downstage, the while, in total silence and in the proverbial agony of suspense. It worked very well that way, and I cannot
believe Shakespeare intended it any other way.

There is not much doubt in my mind that, if the Duke ever felt
that he was involved in a play, he would be pretty sure that it was
reaching its climax now. Mariana has acceded to the bed-trick and
the rest is now, barring accidents, a formality. Indeed he arrives in
the prison to greet the provost in outrageously good spirits, determined, once Isabella has arrived with the pardon, to bring Angelo to
book in the strictest secrecy. From 4.2.79 he is maintaining the
moral duality of the friar/Duke more fiercely than ever. But it is the
further treachery of Angelo at 4.2.120 that raises the play onto an
altogether different plane. It is this, I am convinced, that determines
him to make it a public trial. Fuelled by a white-hot fury at Angelo's
behaviour, together with the necessity, as he now sees it, to turn the
issue into a moral crusade to save the city, it is this, hand in hand
with the drums of the suspense thriller beating around him with
ever greater insistence, that gives this section of the play its wonderful tension. The play is working now on so many levels.

And the Duke's first line at 4.2.129: 'What is that Barnardine who
is to be executed in the afternoon?', which follows directly upon the
provost's reading of Angelo's instructions, brings confirmation of the
way Shakespeare means the play to go in this last phase. No puzzle-
ment, no sense of pulling himself together, not even shock or out-
rage. The response is unequivocal and ruthlessly unemotional. He is
out to get his man and nothing will deflect him. There are far wider
implications now that simply have to be faced. For the Duke it is a
stunning moment of self-discovery—'What is that Barnardine?'—a
growl of steely resolution in the mind.

Indeed he spends the rest of the scene steamrollering the provost.
He simply will not be denied. There is no time to lose. There is some
fun in it too. Here again, I must say that playing this scene with
Oliver Ford-Davies's wonderfully impregnable provost was the purest
pleasure, and, of course, by the next scene at 4.3.74, the provost,
though he doesn't quite know why yet, is warming to the exigencies
of the plot by coming up with the brilliant ploy of recommending the

him is that he has, in him, a tremendous force for good and, even more importantly, the strength with which to implement it. In a sense, perhaps unconsciously, he sets the play in motion in order to discover this. The excitement for him lies in the fact that it was there all the time.

When mercy has such thoughts and feelings behind it, one begins to see lines like 'O, I will to him and pluck out his eyes' in a very different light. You cease, in a curious way, to be involved in the specific moment. You are looking to the future, towards resolution. I see in the margin of my script for this scene in Act 4 with Isabella, the words: 'He learns the efficacy of harshness. An indispensable quality for any ruler. Existential as well as Christian.'

Shakespearean fifth acts are notoriously difficult to stage. The various strands of the plot come together, each one thirsty for resolution, the stage is suddenly chock-a-block with people; where to put them, how best to focus them. In the case of *Measure for Measure*, of course, practically the entire city of Vienna is there. I thought Adrian Noble was triumphant here. He, together with Bob Crowley and Ilona Sekacz with her music, created a theatrical image that swept the play into its final pages with a combination of suspense, theatricality, and danger that served the play perfectly. I derived enormous pleasure from working with Adrian. His ideas are theatrically bold and brave, both intellectually and emotionally. He shares his experience of the play with you and invites you to share yours with him. It is this that gives the work its freedom, and breeds the confidence with which to project it. With Shakespeare confidence is everything. What I find difficult to accept in a director is arbitrary imposition. That is the handmaiden of fear, unreasoning fear, that most destructive of all human emotions. I certainly hope that the reader will accept that, for reasons of space, I have not always been able to celebrate the fact that almost everything discussed in this essay is the result of fruitful and fascinating debate between the two of us. I thank him gratefully.

But quite apart from the staging problems, the fifth act requires enormously concentrated playing, accounted for by the number of levels on which the play is operating. The stage is now peopled by accomplices to the Duke's scheme, some who know about the plot and some who don't. Preparations have been made before the Duke arrives, of which he is, of course, keenly aware. He is aware, too, as they are, that to succeed, the plan must work to the precision of a watch. And it is vital that all those who both *do not* know and *should not* know, MUST NOT KNOW what is going on. As if this were not enough to be going on with, it is clear that if the scheme goes according to plan, it will affect the psychological state of the main protagonists in ways that are subtle, grave, and complex.

and the Duke hurries away to find himself or, more truthfully, to make the fastest quick change in theatrical history. But back he comes. One notices, instantly, that there is some similarity in tone to the Duke's. In any event he is as strident and outraged in the friar's behalf, as he was in the Duke's. Again, to the sharper ear, things are a shade over dramatized. He has, however, points to make, and more importantly, objectives to achieve. He must unmask himself. He does achieve this at line 355, when, in the middle of a crowd of spectators, Lucio finally tears the cowl from his head.

At last. I remember I used to long for this moment in performance. The design so far has worked wonderfully well. But it is the integrity of this moment for which he has worked so hard. He is not to be disappointed. The tone changes here again, of course, reflected in the natural unforced tone of authority. No false histrionics. The rage and pain are specific though:

> Sir, by your leave.
> Hast thou or word, or wit, or impudence,
> That yet can do thee office? If thou hast,
> Rely upon it till my tale be heard,
> And hold no longer out.   (lines 362–6)

The drive of the scheme continues unabated, however, always thinking ahead:

> DUKE   Come hither, Mariana.
>   Say: Wast thou e'er contracted to this woman?
> ANGELO   I was, my lord.
> DUKE   Go take her hence, and marry her instantly.
>   Do you the office, friar, which consummate,
>   Return him here again. Go with him, Provost.

Then:

> ESCALUS   My Lord, I am more amaz'd at his dishonour
>   Than at the strangeness of it.
> DUKE   Come hither, Isabel.
>   (lines 374–81)

It is a fascinating sequence. Short, sharp commands that leave no room for protest, Escalus's remark rudely thrust aside. There are important matters to hand.

Even with Isabella, there is a genuine and felt simplicity, marvel though one does at the superb control and nerve of the deception. There is always the importance of completing the task the speech sets out to perform:

> DUKE   Make it your comfort,
>   So happy is your brother.   (lines 398–9)

DUKE   Your suit's unprofitable; stand up, I say.
    I have bethought me of another fault.
    Provost, how came it Claudio was beheaded
    At an unusual hour?   (lines 453–8)

He cannot wait now to spring the rabbit out of the hat. Having
despatched the provost, he stands, eyes fixed unblinkingly on Angelo,
waiting, the stage still holding the trance-like tension of Isabella's
capitulation. Then into the focussed pool of light, the provost appears
with these two muffled men.

DUKE   Which is that Barnardine?
PROVOST   This, my lord.

A pardon, for the first time. Is this an intimation of things to come?
A stirring among the crowd, and then:

DUKE   What muffled fellow's that?
PROVOST   This is another prisoner that I sav'd,
    Who should have died when Claudio lost his head,
    As like almost to Claudio as himself.   (lines 486–9)

And with that, the provost slowly draws the sacking from his head,
shaved now, of course, from the experience of prison, his eyes slowly
blinking their unaccustomed way into light, the head beginning to
turn, a look of puzzled disorientation on his face. Then, gradually, he
and those around him begin to realize the miracle of what they are seeing in each other. For the Duke it is a secret he has held right through
the play, a talisman, but much more importantly a potent symbol of the
magical properties of mercy. Even here, though, he moves on:

DUKE (*to* ISABELLA)   If he be like your brother, for his sake
    Is he pardon'd, and for your lovely sake,
    Give me your hand, and say you will be mine.   (lines 490–2)

It is important to remember, I think, that the image of Claudio coming magically to life remains in the energy of the play as a very
potent force, for the rest of its duration. I think it will exist in the life
of the whole city for years to come, developing, perhaps, the properties of a mythological story. In any event, one's playing of the scene
was hugely influenced by it, not to mention the audience's response.

My proposal there to Isabella often used to get a laugh. I never
minded. There is more than a little chutzpah involved in the timing of
it anyway. It is nothing more nor less than autocratic licence. One
must surrender to that full-bloodedly.

Indeed, I think the coda of the play should be seen almost as if the
Duke is settling his accounts with himself, his city, and his subjects.
In a very real sense he is celebrating the re-establishment of an
autocracy. There are instructions for all, including himself:

or what it should be. It is astonishing, therefore, to learn that the bed-trick appears in at least forty-four plays of the period and is used by most of the major Stuart dramatists. Middleton uses the bed-trick at least five times. Shakespeare uses it in four plays, as does Shirley. Marston, Fletcher, Heywood, and Brome each use the bed-trick in three plays, while Massinger, Chapman, Dekker, and Rowley each use it in one. The only major dramatist who does not use the bed-trick is Ben Jonson, and he uses two related conventions of partner substitution: the boy bride of *Epicoene* and the substituted groom of *The Alchemist*. Clearly, the substitution of one partner for another, particularly the sexual substitution of the bed-trick, served important dramatic purposes for the playwrights, and their contin-ued use of the convention suggests that it had significant emotional resonances for their audiences as well.

Critical discussions of this convention agree on the basic action that underlies the bed-trick: a sexual encounter occurs in which at least one partner is unaware of the other partner's true identity. The deceived person had expected someone else and, because the couple meet in the dark, he or she fails to detect the substitution. With this basic definition, however, critical agreement about bed-tricks ends, and critical dissension begins over what the bed-trick ends, and crit-ical dissension begins over what the bed-trick signifies and how En-glish Renaissance audiences would have responded to it. This focus on the original audiences' responses has, in turn, become a major issue in arguments about how modern audiences "ought" to respond to bed-tricks. Amid these arguments, we lose sight of a question that may be more germane: How do modern audiences respond to this convention? All of these issues are of crucial importance if we are to arrive at an understanding of the bed-trick within its English Ren-aissance context and to appreciate it within our modern one. Not surprisingly, most of these issues occupy a central position in the three major critical approaches to defining the bed-trick.

In the first of these, the bed-trick is viewed as little more than an ungraceful, but thoroughly Renaissance, means that Shakespeare uses for resolving plot complications while ignoring psychological reality. John Wain describes it as a "tedious and artificial plot device," which he concedes has some thematic justification in *All's Well That Ends Well* and *Measure for Measure*, although he confidently asserts that "we know that in 'real' life Angelo and Bertram would have soon rec-ognized the girls [*sic*] they were lying beside."[2] Similarly, Jonas Bar-ish finds the bed-trick acceptable in folklore but "too mechanical an

---

2. John Wain, *The Living World of Shakespeare: A Playgoer's Guide* (London: Macmillan and Co., Ltd.; New York: St. Martin's Press, 1964), pp. 102–3.

real life use of the bed-trick during the period, described in Francis Osborne's *Memories*, in which "the last great *Earle of Oxford*, whose *Lady* was brought to his bed under the notion of his *Mistris*, and from such a virtuous deceit she [sc. Pembroke's wife] is said to proceed."[7] Although R. C. Bald, unlike Hunter, does not attempt to cite real life occurrences, he, like Hunter, also argues for Renaissance audiences' equanimity in accepting the bed-trick by stating that "the substitution, or 'bed-trick' as it has been called, would not have been regarded as a mean and rather offensive piece of deception; it was the means by which the injured heroine had won her rights against the man who had wronged her."[8] For these critics, therefore, the bed-trick is to be accepted and not questioned, which is, they assure us, how Renaissance audiences would have responded to it. Any discomfort modern playgoers might feel about the bed-trick is dismissed as anachronistic.

The last of these critical approaches to the bed-trick is less concerned with the issue of psychological probability, which dominates the first approach, or with the issue of contemporary beliefs, which dominates the second. Instead, this third approach stresses the bed-trick's theatrical nature. Critics who advocate this approach, however, disagree on whether theatricality implies the deliberate overuse of a worn convention in order to comment on the dramatic process, or whether theatricality implies deliberate and continual variations of an accepted convention in order to entertain. William Baille, discussing the bed-trick in *Grim the Collier of Croydon*, asserts that the dramatist "wrings new comic life out of a stale convention."[9] Ann Slater, referring to Shakespeare's use of it in the problem plays, calls the bed-trick "a stale theatrical ruse."[1] Margot Heinemann, John Pentzell, and John McElroy, all writing on *The Changeling*, respectively dub the bed-trick "a commonplace of the drama,"[2] "that old warhorse of romance,"[3] and "that hoary veteran of all kinds of drama."[4]

7. G. K. Hunter, introduction to *All's Well That Ends Well* (London: Methuen & Co., Ltd., 1959; reprinted, with minor corrections, 1962), p. xliv. Hunter credits this reference to Edgar I. Fripp, who gives it in *Shakespeare, Man and Artist* (1938), 2, p. 601. The passage is from the 1658 edition of Osborne's *Memoires*, p. 79.
8. R. C. Bald, introduction to *Measure for Measure*, in *William Shakespeare: The Complete Works*, ed. Harbage, p. 400.
9. William M. Baille, introduction to *Grim the Collier of Croydon, A Choice Ternary of English Plays* (Binghamton, N.Y.: Medieval & Renaissance Texts & Studies, 26, 1984), p. 184.
1. Ann Pasternak Slater, *Shakespeare the Director* (Sussex: The Harvester Press; Totowa; N.J.: Barnes & Noble Books, 1982), p. 151.
2. Margot Heinemann, *Puritanism and Theatre: Thomas Middleton and Opposition Drama under the Early Stuarts* (Cambridge: Cambridge University Press, 1980), p. 176.
3. Raymond J. Pentzell, "*The Changeling*: Notes on Mannerism in Dramatic Form," *Drama in the Renaissance: Comparative Critical Essays*, ed. Clifford Davidson, C. J. Gianakaris, and John H. Stoupe (New York: AMS Press, 1986), p. 280.
4. John F. McElroy, *Parody and Burlesque in the Tragicomedies of Thomas Middleton*, Jacobean Drama Studies 19 (Salzburg Studies in English Literature, Salzburg, 1972), p. 85. It is unclear whether McElroy's pun is intentional.

ences would have experienced no emotional discomfort in seeing a bed-trick on stage. One difficulty with this approach is that whether we like it or not we belong to modern audiences, and many of us do feel uncomfortable.[8] And how are we to know that at least some members of those original audiences did not share that discomfort? To claim that they unanimously accepted the bed-trick without a second thought is to claim a unanimity in their society's attitudes that has yet to be found in any society's in any historical period. London playgoers may well have had varied emotional reactions to the bed-trick, and despite Hunter's reference to one real life bed-trick—an interesting case of life's imitating art—there is little indication that bed-tricks were part of social practice. The greatest draw-back to this historical approach, however, is that while it purports to deal exclusively with the prevailing attitudes of a given society, it actually measures those supposed attitudes against modern ones which are usually held up as superior. To assert, therefore, as Hunter does, that English Renaissance society saw marriage as "social convenience" rather than as "personal emotion" and so would consider the bed-trick "a smaller violation of the spirit of marriage than we can today" is to judge by modern Western beliefs that discount the possibility of love in arranged marriages. Cultural differences do exist between our society and that of Renaissance England, and we need to recognize them, but we should be cautious in how we interpret those differences. A historical approach is valuable in an examination of the bed-trick only if it first focuses on the historical theatrical use of the convention, and only then on the social implications that might be inferred from that context. Those inferences will, in turn, be limited by the theatrical context, which may reflect tensions within a society, but which does not necessarily reflect a mirror image of society.

While the third approach does emphasize the bed-trick's dramatic usefulness, it all too often ignores this historical theatrical context. Most advocates of this approach base their conclusions on very few plays, even though they stress that the bed-trick is in common use on the stage throughout the period. Because they wish to focus on self-conscious elements in the drama, and that is a legitimate line of

---

8. The critical approaches I am discussing exemplify this discomfort in that the writers feel compelled to offer elaborate explanations of, or apologies for, the bed-trick to modern audiences. We see similar discomfort in our undergraduate students who, like the boy in Anderson's fairy tale who points out the emperor's lack of clothing, brush such explanations aside and question the bed-trick's acceptability. In addition, the discomfort manifests itself in other ways. These range from complete rejection of the bed-trick as an acceptable dramatic device, to expressions of nervous anxiety (such as laughter), to attempts to dismiss the bed-trick as a mere device in order not to have to deal with its more disturbing implications. While it is true that we cannot measure emotional responses such as "anxiety" and "discomfort" with scientific objectivity, that does not mean that we should ignore or discount their existence.

help to explain why it has been the focus of repeated critical attempts to explain it away.

*   *   *

Nearly 20 percent of bed-tricks in English Renaissance drama occur within the context of established marriages. This fact suggests that the dramatists found it a useful device for exploring marital relationships and, in the case of wives who use it to reform their husbands, a way of dramatizing a widespread cultural fantasy about the role of a wife. In dealing with matters of marriage, however, the dramatists were also aware that the bed-trick can be a useful device for exploring the making of marriages. Although the bed-trick in the context of betrothal or precontract was not widely used by the dramatists, there are at least four instances of this kind of bed-trick, the most famous of these, and possibly the first, being that of *Measure for Measure* (1604).

Discussions of the bed-trick in *Measure for Measure* almost inevitably get bogged down in matters of the legal status of betrothals and whether or not sexual relations before the consecration of a marriage were considered acceptable in Shakespeare's age. J. W. Lever sums up the pertinent information on this complex subject:

> English common law recognized two forms of "spousals". *Sponsalia per verba de praesenti*, a declaration by both parties that each took the other at the present time as spouse, was legally binding irrespective of any change of circumstances, and, whether the union was later consecrated or not, amounted to full marriage. *Sponsalia per verba de futuro*, a sworn declaration of intention to marry in the future, was not thus absolutely binding. Failure of certain conditions to materialize, notably failure to furnish the agreed dowry, justified a unilateral breach.[3]

When Mariana's dowry is lost, Angelo is thus within his rights to end the betrothal. As Joyce Youings points out, "promises made in the future tense, especially if conditional on parental consent or on settlement of land or goods, were not binding, unless followed by intercourse."[4] Although this historical background is often cited to justify Mariana's participation in the bed-trick, there is actually no legal endorsement for the bed-trick itself but only a legal description of what the status of the couple would be after consummation. When Vincentio declares to Mariana that Angelo "is your husband on a pre-contract," and argues that "the justice of your title to him / Doth

---

3. J. W. Lever, introduction to *Measure for Measure*, pp. liii–liv. Further references to this
    edition appear in the text.
4. Joyce Youings, *Sixteenth-Century England* (New York: Penguin, 1984), p. 362.

she causes the sexual responses that various men have toward her. Isabella also subscribes to this belief, and she is so frightened of this supposed power that she seeks a life away from men in an order of nuns with very strict rules. Although critics often focus on Isabella's "repressed" sexuality as her personal shortcoming, she is actually very much a product of a society that views female sexuality negatively and often fearfully.[6] While Isabella has been criticized for repressed sexuality, Mariana has been criticized for agreeing so readily to the bedtrick, or else for being so devoted to Angelo whose "unjust unkindness," as Vincentio puts it, "in all reason should have quenched her love," instead of "like an impediment in the current, made it more violent and unruly" (3.1.240–43). Once again, the issue is the negative sexual power this society ascribes to women and the lack of actual power it gives them to right the wrongs committed against them. When Angelo broke his engagement to Mariana after her dowry and her brother were lost at sea, he did so not on the grounds that the dowry was a condition for the marriage but by "pretending in her discoveries of dishonour" (3.1.226–27). He has destroyed her reputation, and with the male relative who would have defended her honor dead, a point that undoubtably influenced the manner in which Angelo rejected her, she has no means to clear her name.[7] Since no other man will marry a woman with a damaged reputation, her only hope if she wishes to marry and to regain the place in society that Angelo's

---

6. Such a society maintains a polarized attitude toward women: women are either idealized or looked upon with sexual loathing. The result for women is a very confusing message about sexuality. We can also detect similar attitudes in the critics' responses to Isabella. Jacqueline Rose makes the case most cogently:

> Isabella is not the only "problem" in this play . . . but criticism has alternatively revered and accused her in such a way that her sexual identity has become the site on which dissatisfaction with the play, and disagreement about the play, have turned. No character in the play has produced a "wider divergence of opinion" (R. M. Smith 1950, p. 212), opinions which, despite the differences between them, once again have in common their *excess*. Isabella has been the object of "excessive admiration" and "excessive repugnance" (Smith, p. 212), uniting in her person those extremes of attraction and recoil which were latent in T. S. Eliot's comparison of the *Mona Lisa* with *Hamlet*. Strangely, the accusations against Isabella have, if anything, been stronger than those against Gertrude, suggesting that it is the desire provoked by the woman which is above all the offence, and that the woman who refuses to meet that desire is as unsettling as the one who does so with excessive haste. Isabella has been described as a "hussy" (Charlton, *cit.* R. M. Smith 1950, p. 213), "hysterical" (Lever, Introduction to Arden ed., Shakespeare 1965, p. lxxx), as suffering "inhibition" (Knight 1930, p. 102) or "obsession" (Jardine 1983, p. 192) about sex. She has also been revered as divine. The two positions are, however, related and the second can easily tip over into the first. Angelo himself makes the link: "Shall we desire to raze the sanctuary / And pitch our evils there?" "What is't I dream on? / O cunning enemy, that, to catch a saint, / With saints dost bait thy hook!" (II.ii.171–72, 180–82).

See "Sexuality in the Reading of Shakespeare," in *Alternative Shakespeares,* ed. John Drakakis (London: Methuen, 1985), pp. 103–4.

7. That the death of Mariana's brother influences the manner of Angelo's rejection of her can be seen in his later statement as to why he orders Claudio's execution after Isabella apparently has given into his demands:

ADAPTATIONS AND RESPONSES

WILIAM D'AVENANT

From The Law against Lovers†

*Act 4, Scene 1. Enter * * * Angelo and Isabella.*

* * *

ISAB   Can I when free, be by your words subdu'd,
    Whose actions have my Brother's life pursu'd?
ANG   I never meant to take your Brother's life'
    But in trial how to chuse a wife,
    I have been too diffident, to curious been,
    I'll pardon ask for folly, as for sin;
    I lov'd you e're your pretious beauties were
    In your probation shaded at Saint *Clare*:
    And when with sacred Sisterhood confin'd,
    A double enterprise perplex my mind;
    By *Claudio*'s danger to provoke you forth
    From that blest shade, and then to try your worth.
ISAB   She that can comply with such a sudden change,
    Has mighty faith, and kindness too so strong,
    That the extream cannot continue long.
    I am so pleas'd with *Claudio*'s liberty,
    That the example shall preserve me free. * * *
    I wish your love so violent and true,
    That those who shall hereafter curious be,
    To seek that frailty, which they would not see,
    May by your punishment become afraid,
    To use those Nets which you ignobly laid.

Act 5, Scene 1. Enter Duke and Isabel, * * *
Lucio, * * * Balthasar, * * * Benedick, * * * Angelo

DUKE   You told me, Daughter that the Marshal has
    Your Brother's pardon seal'd, and I shall watch
    All means to keep him safe, lest *Angelo*
    Should turn his clemency into revenge.
    Do not th'assurance of his freedom buy
    With hazard of a Virgins liberty.

---

† From *The Works of Sir William Davenant* (London: Printed by T. N. for Henry Herring-man, 1673), pp. 315–16, 325, 328–29. This play is adapted from *Measure for Measure* and *Much Ado about Nothing*.

Your Pris'ners free. The story of this day,
When 'tis to future Ages told, will seem
A moral drawn from a poetick Dream.

FINIS

CHARLES GILDON

From Measure for Measure,
or, Beauty the Best Advocate[†]

Act 3, Scene 1. *The Prison.*
Enter Duke, Fryer, * * * *Isabella*

* * *

DUKE   You've heard of *Mariana*, *Frederick*'s Sister,
  Who, with her Brother, lost her Hopes and Fortune.
ISA   Both sunk at Sea, or I mistake.
DUKE   Ev'n so.—This *Angelo*, then but low in Fortune,
  In *Frederick*'s Absence won this Maid to love him.
  And fearing *Frederick*'s Aversion to the Match
  Shou'd hinder him from doing what he'd promis'd,
  Marry'd her in private, none being by
  But his own Creatures: but that same Day
  News came of *Frederick*'s Ship being cast away,
  And with it, him, and all her Hopes of Wealth.
ISA   Thus far how like my Brother's State!
DUKE   But no farther. This sordid Man convey'd
  Away all proof of what was done,
  And thus has left her a poor mournful Widow,
  Maid and Wife.
ISA   O. base ungrateful Villain!
DUKE   She loves him still, ungrateful as he is:
  Go you again then to Lord Angelo:
  Seem as if won, and make the dark Appointment.
  She shall supply your Place: the Act is just
  And innocent, and must save your Brother.
ISA   But is he marry'd?
FRYER   We both assure you that: You sure may trust us.

---

† From *Measure for Measure, or Beauty the Best Advocate, written originally by Mr. Shakespear:*
  And now very much Alter'd [by Charles Gildon]; *With Additions of Several Entertainments of*
  MUSICK (London: Printed for D. Brown & R. Parker, 1700), pp. 25, 28–30, 34, 44.

* * *

CLAU   Like a good Play, our first Act promis'd wonders,
But the false Deputy and Miser *Pedro,*
With envious guilty hands pulls down the Curtaine,
And spightfully forbid the rest.
Oh! *Julietta,* how canst thou forgive me?
The cursed cause of this thy shameful woe?

JUL   Oh! rather how can'st thou forgive me, *Claudio?*

Act 5, Scene 1. The Great Hall in the Palace

Enter ANGELO, *and* ESCALUS, * * * DUKE, * * *
ISABELLA, * * * MARIANA, * * * PROVOST,
CLAUDIO, *and* JULIETTA

* * *

DUKE   Is this that *Bernardine* that you have sav'd?

PROV   It is, my Liege, as like to *Claudio* as himself.

DUKE   If he be like your Brother he is safe.

ISA   My Brother!

CLAU   My Sister!   *They embrace.*

DUKE   Give me your hand, and say you will be mine,
He is my Brother too, but fitter time for that. * * *

ESCALUS   My Liege, before you do retire, I beg of you
To share the joy we have for your return:
The sudden notice crampt our zeal to this.

DUKE   If Isabella please we all will share it.
Come sit by me. I know thy Vertue Royal,
Thy House as ancient as thy Beauty's young.
They all sit. The last Musick.

The Fourth Entertainment

Phebus Rises in his Chariot over the Sea. The *Nercides* out of
the Sea. * * *

(BISHOP, ANGELO   repeat: *Love you. Wronged you while*
    CLAUDIO's *voice crescendos above it.*)
CLAUDIO   Let me live. Let me live. Let me live!!!
ISABELLA   Dissolve my life, let not my sense unsettle
    Lest I should drown, or stab, or hang myself.
    O state of Nature, fail together in me
    Since the best props are warpt. So which way now?
    The best way is the next way to a grave.
    Each errant step beside is torment. Lo,
    The moon is down, the crickets chirp, the screech-owl
    Calls in the dawn. All offices are done
    Save what I fail in.
    An end, and that is all.

Lights blend surreally. CLAUDIO *suddenly appears.* ISABELLA *rushes into his arms. They embrace desperately.* CLAUDIO *takes her by the hand and leads her towards the curtained-bed. There she is presented to* ANGELO *who clasps* CLAUDIO's *hand as* CLAUDIO *does his.* ANGELO *then motions for* CLAUDIO *to depart.* CLAUDIO *begins to back out of the scene and into the waiting arms of the* PROVOST *who smiles curiously at* CLAUDIO *then, putting his arm around his shoulder in a fraternal manner, leads him out.*

ISABELLA *stands mute and still.* ANGELO *approaches her and tenderly undoes her nun's headpiece.* ISABELLA's *short, cropped hair is revealed underneath. Then he undoes her nun's habit until she stands naked before him. She remains still and devoid of emotion. Then,* ANGELO *bends down, places his arms around her waist and his head in the pit of her stomach.*

Instinctively, ISABELLA *makes a move as if to embrace* ANGELO's *head, but the gesture is cut short, and she then resumes her neutral position.* ANGELO *lifts her into his arms, draws open the surrounding curtains, and disappears behind them with* ISABELLA. *Downstage, in a gloomy light, the* BISHOP *appears before* CLAUDIO, *who is kneeling before him, and administers the last rites.*

BISHOP   (*As if intoning a prayer*)
    Be absolute for death: either death or life
    Shall thereby be the sweeter. Reason thus with life. * * *

* * *

ANGELO   I did but smile till now.
    Now, good my lord, give me the scope of justice.
    My patience here is touched. I do perceive
    These poor informal wretches are no more

content to be a lawful hangman. I would be glad to receive some instruction from me fellow partner.

ESCALUS   (*Laughing at* ANGELO's *imitation: mock-astonished*) A bawd, sir? (*To* DUKE.) Fie upon him, he will discredit our mystery.

ANGELO   'Faith my lord, I spoke it but according to the trick. If you hang me for it, you may. But I had rather it would please you I might be whipped.

(*All fall about with laughter.*)

DUKE   Whipped first, sir, and hanged after (*This tops last joke and all explode with even greater laughter.*) Proclaim it, Provost around the city,
If any woman wronged by this lewd fellow,
As I have heard him swear himself there's one
Whom he begot with child—let her appear,
And he shall marry her.

ANGELO   (*Acting craven*) I beseech your highness, do not marry me to a whore. Marrying a punk, my Lord, is pressing to death, whipping *and* hanging.

DUKE   (*Pouring wine over* ANGELO's *head*)
Slandering a prince deserves it.

(*All laugh uproariously and carry on clowning, eating and drinking through.*)

(*Fade out*)

[The End]

Selected Bibliography

A basic search in an online bibliography database reveals over seven hundred items of criticism on *Measure for Measure*; a more complex search would offer dozens more. Criticism of the play shifted sharply in the 1970s from the main approaches, through its characters, issues of morality and Christianity, and the "problem comedy" genre to gender study, sexuality, cultural studies, and new historicism. Also in the 1970s came a shift in theater performance, in which sexuality was sometimes explicitly staged and a feminist Isabella rejects, rather than silently accepts, the patriarchal's Duke's proposal at the end of Act 5. In sum, the play is now seen on the stage and as a literary text as subversive and transgressive, marking a turning point in Shakespeare's career, in which he deliberately satirized his earlier "festive" comedies ending in joyous marriages and a restoration of moral order.

In addition to searching online databases, readers can examine a full range of criticism of the play since the eighteenth century by consulting the following printed resources: *Shakespeare: The Critical Heritage, Vols. 1–6*, edited by Brian Vickers (London: Routledge, 1974–81), and *Shakespeare: The Critical Tradition: Measure for Measure*, edited by George L. Geckle (London: Athlone, 2001). Biographies of Shakespeare, such as the standard work, Samuel Shoenbaum's *Shakespeare's Lives* (Oxford University Press, 1979), can shed light on his life during the time in which he was composing *Measure for Measure*. These may also prove useful: Park Honan, *Shakespeare: A Life* (Oxford: Clarendon, 1998); Katherine Duncan-Jones, *Ungentle Shakespeare* (London: Arden Shakespeare, 2001); Stephen Greenblatt, *Will in the World: How Shakespeare Became Shakespeare* (New York: Norton, 2004); and Peter Ackroyd, *Shakespeare: The Biography* (London: Chatto & Windus, 2005).

The following selected bibliography offers some seminal books and articles that can lead readers to a much more broad range of general or specific criticism of *Measure for Measure*. Texts excerpted in the Criticism section of this Norton Critical Edition are not listed here.

Critical Anthologies, Casebooks, and Study Guides

George L. Geckle, *Twentieth Century Interpretations of Measure for Measure: A Collection of Critical Essays* (Englewood Cliffs, N.J.: Prentice-Hall, 1970); Kenneth Muir and Stanley W. Wells, *Aspects of Shakespeare's 'Problem Plays': Articles Reprinted from Shakespeare Survey* (Cambridge: Cambridge University Press, 1982); Kate Chedgzoy, *William Shakespeare: Measure for Measure* (Plymouth, UK: Northcote House, with British Council, 2000).

Contemporary Theater and Culture

Josephine Waters Bennett, *Measure for Measure as Royal Entertainment* (New York: Columbia University Press, 1966); John Wasson, "*Measure for Measure*: A Text for Court Performance?" *Shakespeare Quarterly* 21 (1970), 17–24; G. Blakemore

Universal Theater: Shakespeare in Performance Then and Now (Chicago: University of Chicago Press, 2007), and Colin Butler, *The Practical Shakespeare: The Plays in Practice and on the Page* (Athens: Ohio University Press, 2005).

Criticism

Genre

Ira Clark, *Rhetorical Readings, Dark Comedies, and Shakespeare's Problem Plays* (Gainesville: University Press of Florida, 2007); Nicholas Marsh, *Shakespeare: Three Problem Plays* (Basingstoke, UK: Palgrave Macmillan, 2003); Vivian Thomas, *The Moral Universe of Shakespeare's Problem Plays* (New York: Routledge, Chapman & Hall; 1991); Murray Krieger, "*Measure for Measure* and Elizabethan Comedy," *PMLA* 66 (1951), 775–84.

Structure, Style and Themes

Karen Cunningham, "Opening Doubts upon the Law: *Measure for Measure*," in *A Companion to Shakespeare's Works, IV: The Poems, Problem Comedies, Late Plays,* edited by Richard Dutton and Jean E. Howard (Malden, Mass.: Blackwell, 2003), pp. 316–32; Fritz Levy, "The Politics of *Measure for Measure*," in *The Shakespearean International Yearbook,* vol. 5 (Aldershot, UK: Ashgate, 2005), pp. 229–39; Michael J. Redmond, "The Politics of Plot: *Measure for Measure* and the Italianate Disguised Duke Play," in *Shakespeare, Italy, and Intertextuality* (Manchester, UK: Manchester University Press, 2004), pp. 158–75; Paul Hammond, "The Argument of *Measure for Measure*," *English Literary Renaissance* 16 (1986), 496–519; Alexander Leggatt, "Substitution in *Measure for Measure*," *Shakespeare Quarterly* 39 (1988), 342–59; Lindsay M. Kaplan, *The Culture of Slander in Early Modern England* (Cambridge: Cambridge University Press, 1997); Dieter Mehl, "Corruption, Retribution and Justice in *Measure for Measure* and *The Revenger's Tragedy*," in *Shakespeare and His Contemporaries: Essays in Comparison,* edited by E. A. J. Honigmann (Manchester, UK: Manchester University Press, 1986), 114–28; E. A. J. Honigman, "Shakespeare's Mingled Yarn and *Measure for Measure*," *Proceedings of the British Academy* 67 (1981), 101–21.

Characters

A. C. Bradley's *Shakespearean Tragedy* (excerpted herein) is the standard reference work on Shakespeare's characters; for some more recent and specific studies see Karl F. Zender, "Isabella's Choice," *Philological Quarterly* 73 (1994), 77–93; Bernice W. Kliman, "Isabella in *Measure for Measure*," *Shakespeare Studies* (1982), 137–48; Cynthia Lewis, "'Dark Deeds Darkly Answered': Duke Vincentio and Judgment in *Measure for Measure*," *Shakespeare Quarterly* 34 (1983), 271–89; Julia Brett, "'Grace Is Grace, Despite of All the Controversy': *Measure for Measure*, Christian Allegory, and the Sacerdotal Duke," *Ben Jonson Journal* 6 (1999): 189–207; Roger Allam, The Duke in *Measure for Measure*, in *Players of Shakespeare 3* edited by Russell Jackson and Robert Smallwood (Cambridge: Cambridge University Press, 1993), 21–41.

Theoretical Approaches

The predominant recent approaches to the play have been feminist and new historicist. See for example Lynda Boose, "The Priest, the Slanderer, the Historian and the Feminist," *English Literary Renaissance* 25 (1995), 320–40; Carol Thomas Neely, "Constructing Female Sexuality in the Renaissance: Stratford, London, Windsor, Vienna," in Richard *Feminism and Psychoanalysis,* edited by Richard Feldstein and Judith Roof (Ithaca, N.Y.: Cornell University Press, 1989), 209–29;

Marriage, Mercy, comic structure
Isabella : female silence
=
Kate's silence

How does the play balance the
demands of the community
w/ the rights of the individual

"remedy"

goal of law?
legislate against crimes
vs severity
or
reform the people
↓
mercy
handfasting